WHAT PEOPLE ARE SAYI]

REIKI: EMPOWERED BY IT, EMBRACED BY IT, CLAIMED BY IT

Robert Levy introduces a fresh and intuitive look at Reiki energy healing offering unique perspectives and useful information for beginning and advanced practitioners alike. He integrates additional effective tools that are designed to enhance your hands-on practice and encourage a personal, creative connection to the Universal Life Force Energy.

Llyn Roberts, M.A., award winning author of *Shapeshifting into Higher Consciousness* and coauthor of *Shamanic Reiki*. www.LlynRoberts.com

In his book Reiki: Empowered By It, Embraced By It, Claimed By It, Robert Levy elegantly escorts us out of the box of traditional Reiki techniques and teaches us how to develop a deep learning relationship with the Divine intelligence of Reiki itself. Mr Levy's valuable work helps make Reiki more accessible and user friendly to all.

Brett Bevell, M.A., author of the books *New Reiki Software for Divine Living, Reiki for Spiritual Healing* and *The Reiki Magic Guide To Self Attunement*

i

Looking Forward

The purpose of this book is to allow you to:

be empowered by Reiki.
be embraced by Reiki.
deepen your connection to Reiki.
relate to Reiki on a personal level.
claim Reiki as Universe's true gift to you.

Within its pages, you will find:
your Reiki,
not my Reiki,
not your teacher's Reiki,
not anyone else's Reiki.

Your Reiki, and
it will be in complete harmony
with your higher self and your divine soul.

Reiki:

Empowered By It, Embraced By It, Claimed By It

Reiki:
Empowered By It,
Embraced By It,
Claimed By It

Robert Levy

AYNI
BOOKS

Winchester, UK
Washington, USA

First published by Ayni Books, 2013
Ayni Books is an imprint of John Hunt Publishing Ltd., Laurel House, Station Approach,
Alresford, Hants, SO24 9JH, UK
office1@jhpbooks.net
www.johnhuntpublishing.com
www.ayni-books.com

For distributor details and how to order please visit the 'Ordering' section on our website.

Text copyright: Robert Levy 2013

ISBN: 978 1 78279 065 5

A CIP catalogue record for this book is available from the British Library.

Design: Lee Nash

Printed in the USA by Edwards Brothers Malloy

We operate a distinctive and ethical publishing philosophy in all
areas of our business, from our global network of authors to
production and worldwide distribution.

CONTENTS

Acknowledgments

There is a concept that all the people we meet on our life's journey are in some way our teachers. I wish to thank all of my teachers who helped me evolve into the Reiki practitioner that I now am. These include my Reiki teachers, my students, my clients, and the friends I made (and lost) who are also Reiki practitioners. They include the many people who I have met along the way who are part of other healing modalities but added to my knowledge of Universe and her generosity to us. To name them all would be impossible. To all, thank you!

To Maria Watson, my editor, my thanks for your trust that what I said should be heard, and for helping me say it in the best possible way.

To my wife, Shigeko,
for being my wife,
for being my rock,
for being my reason.
Without you, nothing would be possible.

Many Reiki practitioners become disillusioned with Reiki early on in their Reiki career.
They are filled with self-doubt.
They wonder if Reiki is valid.
They wonder if Reiki works.

To those of your who have felt like that or to those of you who wish to look at Reiki from a different light, a light that begins within the Heart of Reiki and shines directly on you, filling you with her wonder, her energy, her love, her compassion and her understanding, this book is dedicated.

In the memory of Ipupiara Makunaiman.

Author's note:

Material in this text is for informational purposes. Reiki and medicine are two different modalities. Reiki should be used only as a complimentary discipline. In case of serious illness, please consult a medical practitioner.

B eware - you are about to read a book on Reiki like no other you have read before because I may blatantly blaspheme some of the tenants of Reiki taught by many Reiki Masters. I ask you to read this with an open mind, and if you will, by the time you finish, I promise that the Reiki you practice will not only be more powerful, but it will be completely personal. It will be YOUR Reiki. Not my mine, not your teacher's, but yours. And there will be no attunements and no extra fees, except purchasing his book.

I am sure everyone who is reading this knows that many medicines come in two forms, brand names and generic names. Though most of the time the generic medicines work with equal effectiveness, sometimes they don't and the brand name, selected by a physician on an individual basis, may. Generic may not be for every one.

Reiki can also come in two forms. Generic Reiki, the one everyone learns, and, instead of using the words brand Reiki, I will use the term Personal Reiki, the Reiki prescribed to you alone.

But first, a quick review of Reiki, which I explain as follows:

What is Reiki?

Reiki is a Universal Life Force Energy, a healing gift from Universe to all of us. It requires very little training in the simplest level. It can be performed by anyone who has been attuned and is painless, never harming, and, in my opinion, always relaxing. Though many people consider and refer to Reiki as an alternative medicine, I chose to speak of it as complementary. Alternative can be interpreted as "instead of modern medicine" and complementary would be "used in harmony with modern medicine."

How Do You Perform Reiki?

The Reiki practitioner holds his or her hands either slightly above or gently on, the person receiving Reiki. The practitioner then connects with the Reiki Energy using only the power of his/her intent. The Reiki Energy enters the practitioner, goes through him/her and exits through the hands. The energy then enters the client. But it doesn't stay where the hands are. People from different Reiki schools of thought may argue over many things, but one thing that all practitioners agree on is that Reiki is an intelligent energy. It ought to be since it is a gift from Divine Universe. Therefore, once the energy enters the body, it goes where it is needed. I tell my students that it goes to the place that will give the client's higher self the most benefit.

Attunements

Reiki was discovered or rediscovered by Dr. MIkao Usui. There may be many stories about how this actually transpired, but the one I was told when being attuned to the first level was Dr. Usui went on a mountain and fasted for twenty-one days. He was searching for an ancient hands on healing system long forgotten. On the last day, as he was about to end his fast, a light appeared in the sky, sank down and entered him through his crown Chakra. Within that light were four symbols. Dr. Usui intuitively knew what the symbols meant and how to use them. He achieved divine enlightenment and was attuned by Universe into Reiki. On that day, modern day Reiki was born.

Some argue that this was the true beginning of Reiki while others say that Universe showed him the healing method used thousands of years ago by ancient Buddhist healers. Modern Reiki practitioners love to nit-pic. I don't, and I don't care which answer is correct. It doesn't matter to me because Reiki is Reiki. It exists.

Anyone can do Reiki and the process is simple. In level 1, (there are 3 levels) a Reiki Master attunes people who wish to learn Reiki. The easiest way of explaining attunements is the Reiki Master adjusts their client's energy using the Reiki Energy to accomplish that. That adjustment allows the client to accept Reiki Energy on their own and transmit it to their future clients or themselves. In a one or two day class, the Reiki Master explains the history of Reiki, leads the participants in one or more guided meditations, and then, the Reiki Master attunes each person. That simply means that the Reiki Masters, through their own visualizations and imagination, and acting as Universe's agent, place into each of their students, some of the symbols Universe gave Dr. Usui. This is done in several locations and not all the symbols are given in each location. This is the main part of each attunement.

Depending on the Reiki Masters' tradition and beliefs, they may give their students more than one attunement during the Reiki I workshop. In this case, they usually only place one of the symbols into their students for each attunement. If they are giving a two-day workshop, there is ample time for this. Or, they may only give one attunement; placing all the symbols they intend give at one time, which is what I do. Both methods are equally effective.

Following that, the participants practice giving Reiki to each other. The Reiki Master shows the participants the hand positions that many of the Masters consider mandatory, though they are simple enough and should not concern anyone reading this.

In Reiki II, the process is the same except that most of the symbols are placed in all of the locations. Participants are shown three of the four symbols, are told their function and how to use them. There is only one attunement for Reiki II and Reiki III.

Reiki III is more difficult. Aside from placing all the symbols in all locations, the main reason for Reiki III, or Master Level, is for the participants to become Reiki Masters themselves, learn how to attune people, and begin to teach others. In this workshop, the Reiki Master goes into detail how the various attunements are done and what the process is for visualizing the symbols as they enter the participants.

I believe that what I have just said concerning Reiki is the general rule. And yet, it is a one size fits all, Generic Reiki. I assume that most Reiki Masters do as I have explained, teaching their students about what I have outlined and telling them that when they attain Level 3, they should do as they were taught. My question is . . . (but wait, let me offer you a simple analogy).

Christmas or Hanukkah (or any other holiday that you need to buy gifts for) is approaching and you have eight people on your list. They are all different ages and genders. Would you give each the same gift? Would you just order the same sweater, in the same color but in different sizes for everyone? This would be generic gift giving - one gift for everyone. Or, since you care enough about each to give them a gift, would you put some thought into your gift buying and based on the individual prefer- ences of each person, by eight different gifts. This would be personal gift giving.

As I started before, my question is, do you think Universe, in her ultimate wisdom, would present humanity with the wonderful gift of Reiki and then dictate that everyone use it and practice it in exactly same way? For me, the answer is no. Each of us is an individual and when transmitting Reiki, the Universal Life Force Energy must take into account our individual differ- ences. Reiki is not a static energy but a fluid one. My Reiki is my personal healing system, based on my relationship with Universe and the gift she gave me. And her gift to me is not generic. It is a personal. That is the reason this book was written - to show you how to connect directly with the Reiki Energy and claim the personal gift I believe you are entitled to.

Empowerment

Reiki should empower both the practitioner and client, and unfortunately, in its purest form, I do not believe that is always the case. The wonderful thing about Reiki is once you connect with it, the Universal Energy begins to flow through you and into the client. Sometimes, the practitioner may feel the energy releasing from his/her hands in the form of heat, coolness, and itch or tingles. We each experience it in our own way and there is no right way to perceive the energy. Sometimes the client feels the same, and many times the client will ask at the end of a session why the practitioner's hand were so hot.

But sometimes, neither practitioner nor client feels anything. This too can be normal. However, the energy is still flowing. If a practitioner, while giving Reiki, thinks about completing his/her grocery list or about a sick friend or trying to remember if a TV show that is on now is being recorded, it doesn't matter.

The Reiki Energy is flowing.

The reason for this is, and this is very important, we, as Reiki practitioners, DO NOT DO ANYTHING! The Reiki Energy, the Universal Life Force Energy, does all the work. All we do is stand there, with our hands out, and allow the energy to flow through us. It's that simple.

But knowing that we don't do anything is not empowering. As human beings, especially working in the complimentary healing field of Reiki, we want to feel that we are part of the process.

We want to feel that we, by our actions and intentions, are more than just mannequins letting energy flow through us.

We want to feel that the Reiki Energy acknowledges us for our part, even though that part is small, and is including us while doing her work.

We want to feel that we are One with Reiki.

We want to feel connected to Reiki in a personal way.

We want to feel empowered by Reiki!

By following the meditations in this book, you will attain this feeling of empowerment. You will find the path that leads to a close and personal relationship with Reiki. You will discover your Reiki and claim it as your own. And if you have been attuned to any level of Reiki, even a Reiki Master, and have lost your connection to Reiki, I promise you, this text will show you the way to reconnecting.

Now, let's begin.

Going to the Source of Reiki

Reiki Energy has a source. Somewhere in the "all that is", in the vastness of our Universe, is the source of Reiki. Where the true source is really doesn't matter. Besides, no one knows. What matters is that through your own visualization and imagination, you can reach the source and begin to create your own personal relationship with it.

Within this book, I will guide you through meditations that will show you how to access the information that will allow you to turn generic Reiki into personal Reiki. If you are familiar with the shamanic technique of journeying, consider each meditation a journey or a series of them. Also, after my first introduction to the meditation, I will not repeat getting yourself ready to meditate. I am sure many of you do it already and your own personal preparation is exactly what is needed each time you start. And if not, begin all meditations they way I have explained.

Divine Universe is by far greater than we can imagine. But we cannot communicate with her in ordinary ways. We cannot call information and ask for her telephone number. We cannot Google her to get her address, and we cannot search Facebook to see if she has a page so we can ask her to list us as a friend. We ARE that already. If we weren't, Reiki wouldn't exist. Universe is concerned about our well-being and wishes us to survive our own folly and not become an extinct species.

However, in her wisdom, Divine Universe has created a way for us to communicate directly with Reiki, the Universal Life Force Energy. It is a private, secure, unshakable connection to her. But there is a price for communicating with her. And it may be a huge one for some of you. If you cannot pay the price, then unfortunately, you may never achieve the goal of attaining your personal Reiki.

The price? I think a very reasonable one. You MUST believe and TRUST that the information you receive while meditating is your own personal truth. You will ask the Universal Life Force Energy, you will ask Reiki to help you begin a personal relationship with her. And you must accept that the information you receive will be valid for you. No matter where the information comes from, no matter how vivid your imagination (and imagination it will be), she will not lie to you. If you ask yourself the question, "Is this real or is this my imagination?" I answer now. It doesn't matter. The answers you receive will be your reality. They will be the answers Universe wishes you to have at this time in your life.

When you begin this first meditation after reading the entire process, do not feel that you must do exactly as you read. If while in the meditation your mind begins to wonder in a different direction, follow that direction and ask the questions when you reach your destination. (And yes, you will know when that occurs and who to ask what you must.) Just remember to keep the intent of the meditation in the active part of your mind. Universe knows far more than you or I, and she will lead you to where you should be. Do not think of my meditations as a teacher's direction of, "Do what I tell you." Instead, think of them only as suggestions.

One more item that you should know. By reading the questions that I suggest you discuss with Reiki, you will know the intent of the meditation. You will also realize that there may be too many questions for one sitting. Therefore, I have broken them up into two or three meditations whenever I felt the need to ask everything is great. But how you do it in reality is up to you. You know what you can do far better than I. If you can do one meditation and come away with everything you need, that's fine. Once you know the intent of the meditation, and if you can think of a way to get to the intent completely on your own, then do it your way. If you need to do more than one mediation, that's fine too. I want you to be your own guide as you navigate the path to claiming your Reiki.

In the quiet of your room, with the lights down and if you feel more comfortable with music, playing any meditative music you wish, begin to relax and take several deep breaths. If you sense any tension in your body, release it. Tense your legs and relax them, breathing out as you do and imagine the tension floating off into space. Do the same with your arms. Take a few more deep breaths. And when you breathe out, imagine that any tension or stress that is within you is forced out with each breath. When you are ready, when you feel completely relaxed, imagine yourself rising up through the building and entering the vastness of the sky.

Once there, call out in your mind to Reiki and ask to be guided to its source. For me, this journey is never long, for I visualize a bright circle of light with a defined outline above me. Your journey may be the same or different. It doesn't matter. You may see (or sense) a light like I do. You may see (or sense) a crystal floating in the sky. You may see a disco ball with many facets of glass and it may even be turning slowly. And your light may be further out. It may be a bright star in the middle of the dark void of space.

Whatever it is, it is your light, your Reiki, your source and your beginning.

Imagine approaching that light and pause when you are near it. This is Reiki in its purest form. Ask it for permission to enter, and when you receive it, (no one I have ever worked with was ever refused permission) enter the light. These are my suggestions once you are in the light. Do them or whatever feels natural to you.

First, breathe deeply through your mouth in your real body lying in our reality, and imagine that you are breathing in the energy of pure Reiki in your meditation, in Reiki's reality. Swallow before you breath out through your nose. Feel the energy. Feel the raw power Universe is gifting you with coursing through your real body, flooding into you though your breath. Feel the Energy going to every part of your body. If you are familiar with Chakras, see or sense the light of Reiki going directly to them, warming, cleansing, invigorating. Feel the chills or tingles spreading out all over you. Try to remember that first feeling, that first surge of energy that entered you and the next time you do Reiki on a client or yourself, recall that energy, feel its power, and rejoice as it flows through you. In doing this, you will have a visceral feeling of bringing Reiki into your session.

When you are comfortable being surrounded by Reiki's energy, in your mind's voice, begin a conversation with Reiki, with the light, with the energy. I give you my questions - ask them - ask your own. It doesn't matter. Ask what is in your heart. And your mind's ear will hear the answers. They will not come in a foreign voice but in your own, just as if I were to ask you how much is 2 + 2? You hear the answer in your mind, in your own voice. You will hear, in the same way, the answers to your questions - but remember, you must pay the price. Believe. Trust.

How can I create a personal relationship with you?
What can I do to feel more deeply connected to you?
What must I do to make you part of my life? Not just my Reiki life, but also my whole life?

End here if you must. Next Meditation:

How do you wish me to use you?

Is there anything about you that I am not aware of? If so, what?

Is there anything that I do now when performing Reiki that is not in harmony with my higher self? If yes, what is it and how can I adjust what I do in order to be in harmony with my higher self?

Why do I feel disconnected with you?

When you have completed those questions or your own or a combination of both, or after only one or two questions if you feel that is enough for this first meditation, thank Reiki for allowing you to enter, and gently withdraw from the light. But as you leave, again, try to remember and keep that energy with you as you return to your real body. Once fully grounded and awake, write down everything you learned from this meditation. I suggest you keep a journal of all your meditations since they have a dreamlike quality and you may forget parts of what you have learned.

How many may meditations will it take you to fully merge with and feel completely at ease with the Reiki Energy? I don't know. But you will know and that's all the counts. Remember, it's your journey, your search, and you will know when you are done. If you finish in one meditation, and the questions you asked are sufficient for you, that's fine. If it takes you several, that's fine too. And you may repeat this meditation any time you wish to ask Reiki anything you need to know. The answers are there, waiting for you - all you need to do is ask the questions.

This meditation was the beginning of claiming Universe's gift and making it your own. It was the beginning of learning how to have a personal relationship with Reiki.

Reiki Symbols

Please Note: If you are on the first level of Reiki, you were not introduced to any symbols. However, I want you to do the following meditations anyway. It is very important you do this because I believe that one of the major reasons Level 1 practitioners discontinue their relationship with Reiki and stop practicing it is because they aren't satisfied. This dissatisfaction could be with something they were taught to do, not feeling the flow of Reiki's energy, not seeing positive results or not experiencing Reiki in the way they expected they would. All of these dissatisfactions will be discussed later. But if you do not begin to discover your own personal relationship with the Universal Energy now, at this early stage, there is a good likelihood that your frustration will grow so large you will decide not to continue being a practitioner.

Unfortunately, before you can meditate to the symbols, you have to do a little homework. The assignment is simply to Google "Reiki Symbols." You will find several websites that give you all information you want about them. You will see pictures and you can print them out so you will be able to visualize the symbols in your meditations. What I state below are just the bare bone facts you need to know. You can meditate to the symbols without being attuned to them. And by the time you complete this section, even that may change.

Reiki utilizes symbols. Though there are many different schools of Reiki, including Tibetan Reiki, Karuna Reiki, and Kundalini Reiki, to name a few, in the original Usui Reiki (the one I am attuned to) there are four. These are Cho Ku Rei (Choh-Ku-Ray), Sei He Ki (Say-Hay-Key). Hon Sha Ze Sho Nen (Hon-Shah-Zay-Show-Nen), and Dai Ko Myo (Die-Ko-Me O). Each symbol has a different function. Usui Reiki has always been sufficient for me so I have never pursued any other forms of Reiki. But all forms of Reiki have symbols. Some are the ones I use and some are different. Also, those of you who are not attuned to Reiki Energy at all, but utilize other forms of healing energy, you may have symbols of your own. Though this book is written for Reiki practitioners, the techniques given can be used with any healing system that has its root within Universe's arms. And that covers just about all of them. All you need to do is adapt what you are read to your system. A gift from Universe is a gift from Universe, whether you call it Reiki, Johrei, Quantum-Touch or any other name.

As was told to me and as I told my students, each symbol has a purpose. Those purposes are:

Cho Ku Rei - the power symbol, is used to increase the energy's intensity.

Sei He Ki is used to help in mental and emotional healing.

Hon Sha Ze Sho Nen is used in long distance healing.

Dai Ko Myo is the Master Symbol.

During a Reiki session for the Level 2 and 3 practitioner, the first two symbols may be invoked by the practitioner depending on the nature of the issue. The third symbol is invoked when a practitioner is performing a long distance healing, and either of the first two symbols (or both) may be invoked after the long distance healing symbol. The Master Symbol is usually invoked in the beginning of every session.

I have just told you the generic definitions of the symbols. What I think you should do is find the definitions Universe suggests you to use when invoking them. I want you to personalize them. And as I said before, I believe that even Level 1 practitioners can go to the symbols and receive the information that Reiki wants you to have.

Why do I say it is important for you to meditate on the symbols? You may find a relationship that is different from the generic. I did.

I began my spiritual path in 1995, and after becoming interested in Reiki, I was also curious about different ways to heal others and myself. I became attracted to crystals and crystal healing. I could feel the energy coming from them and I wondered what the function of that energy was. I also knew that different crystals give off different energies and each energy served a different purpose. My teacher was Aimee Morgana, and if she weren't such a sweet and patient mentor, having me as a student would have given her major ulcers. When we went crystal shopping, I would pick up a crystal and say, "What does this one do?" She would tell me what the book said. I bought a book about crystals and even made a list of the crystals I needed because I wanted the energy healing that the book said those crystals possessed.

But then Aimee got tired of me asking all the time. To paraphrase, she said once something like, (and I apologize to her if this is not exactly what she said and how she expressed it, but the thought is the same), "Why are you asking me? Hold the crystal and feel the energy. If you like it, buy it. When you get home, ask the crystal how it can help you. Ask the crystal what its energy can do for you. It doesn't matter what other people say about it, it only matters how you feel about it and what and how the crystal adds to your life."

I did what she said and that was the last time I asked her. That was the beginning of my learning that it was more important to listen to how I felt rather than to listen to what others told me as I began to build the foundation of the Spiritual path I had begun to walk.

When dealing with Universe, many times, people accept the generic (like I did) because that's what most teachers teach. What Aimee wanted me to do was transcend the generic and seek the personal. Many times, the two are the same. But many times, as I found out with my crystals, they are not. I want you to discover for yourself, not only with Reiki, but also with any Spiritual path you happen to find yourself on, what you need to do to build your own foundation. Don't let anyone else, not even me, do that for you.

I offer my own example as to how I know that finding your own definition of the symbols is important. I was asked on several occasions to do long distance Reiki, and that meant invoking the Hon Sha Ze Sho Nen. When I did that type of Reiki, I didn't like doing it. Something was wrong and I was doing it just as I was taught. Then I meditated and went to the symbol. I asked, "What about you is not in harmony with my higher self?" Or to put it another way, "Why don't I feel comfortable doing long distance healing?" The answer was very plain and very simple. I didn't like it because doing it didn't make me feel good. It made me feel like I wasn't doing anything. I would lie on my bed, concentrate on the name of the person and let the Reiki energy flow through me, into a stuffed animal, out into Universe and into my client. Then, after half an hour of doing that, I'd get up and go to the bathroom.

A few more questions - a few more discussions with the symbol and I knew how to claim Hon Sha Ze Sho Nen for myself. From then on, I never just did long distance healing alone. I included my client. At an agreed upon time, when my client would be home, my client would call me.

I wanted them to describe the room they were in and if there were sitting in a chair or lying on a couch or on a bed.

I wanted to be able to visualize both client and location.

I wanted to see in my mind where the Reiki Energy was going.

I wanted my clients to imagine the Reiki Energy entering them.

I wanted both my client and I to feel that we were part of the healing session. I didn't want them to be watching TV or eating dinner or playing tennis and I didn't want to be looking at my watch to see when the half hour was over.

I didn't do many distant healings after that. There were

always lots of excuses why the client wasn't sure about times or places. But the sessions I did do were, for me, deep, meaningful and powerful. When I called the client after the session (or they called me) and we talked, the clients too, were satisfied with the sessions. I felt that all three of us; client, Reiki Energy, and I were working together to bring the healing energy to a person not physically present.

In other words, I felt empowered.

I understood that if a person called and wanted me to do a long distance healing and could not do it the way I chose to do it, they would have to find another practitioner. I know that I may not have been acting in the true spirit of Reiki, turning down a client. But I decided that if I could not do Reiki in a way that was in harmony with who I was, and then I wouldn't do it.

This is an example of turning generic Reiki into a personal Reiki. This is why I believe that discovering what the symbols hold for you is important. You may find that all the symbols have the same meaning you know or read about. Then these meditations will be short and simple. But if you don't ask, then you will always accept the generic Reiki symbols. If you ask, you might discover something that will resonate much more deeply within you just like I did.

Several times in this text I will say what works for me may not work for you. This text is about self-discovery. The Reiki you eventually come up with may parallel mine or be completely different. It doesn't matter which it is as long as it is what you feel and know it should be.

What I suggest you do now are at least four meditations, one for each symbol, but more if you need to visit a symbol twice. If you practice or have been attuned to more than one school of Reiki and have more than four symbols in your basket of knowledge, begin with the symbols that you feel the greatest affinity to.

Again, Level 1 practitioners, please to this. Do these mediations even though the knowledge of the symbols wasn't shared with you. But if you have looked the symbols up on the Internet, you can visualize them. If you read about the symbols, you have the same generic knowledge of their functions just as Level 2 and 3 practitioners do. You CAN do this. I have adjusted the questions I suggested so they will be meaningful to you. But you may ask any questions you wish. You will all get the answers Universe wants you to have.

Imagine a large circle. Everything within it is Reiki. Reiki is more than just; "I put my hands on you and allow the energy to flow through me." By doing the first meditation, you have begun to find out what that "more" is and how it can permeate through your entire life. These symbols are within the circle of Reiki; each is a circle within a circle. They are subsets of Reiki. They are part of, yet, separate. They have their own functions that can only enhance Reiki. What I suggest you do is find out how those symbols can be part of your Reiki and non-Reiki life just as you are beginning to find out how Reiki can be part of your life.

Begin each meditation by returning to the source of Reiki, and once again, ask for permission to enter. When you do, remember the feeling you had the first time you entered the Reiki Energy and try to feel it again. Take all the time you need. Breathe deeply as before and release any tension you feel. When you are ready, begin.

If you have any questions that went unasked during your first visit, ask them now. When you are ready, select one of the four Reiki's symbols. From within the light of Reiki, visualize the symbol as you remember it. It does not matter if you are off in the remembering. Your intention is what fuels the fire of your meditation. Say the symbols name and call it forth. Approach the symbol and again, ask permission to enter.

Notice the feeling you get when entering that symbol. Is it the same feeling you had when you entered the Reiki Energy? If yes, fine - if not - how is it different. If not, try to remember how it is different. Try to put that difference into words and repeat them as many times as you have to in order to remember the difference. Yes, you are stopping the flow of the meditation but it is very important that you remember the difference so you can write it down when the meditation is over.

As I said before, I give you my suggested questions - ask them or ask your own. It still doesn't matter. Continue to ask what's in your heart. And remember, I believe that there might be far more information for just four meditations. By doing this exercise carefully, you continue to build the foundation you need to claim your Reiki.

All levels:

> You are of, yet separate from, Reiki? Why are you necessary? What do you add to Reiki?
>
> What is the best way I can use you in my healing sessions?
>
> Why didn't Universe include you within Reiki? Why was it necessary to separate the functions you perform?
>
> What, if anything, must I do to feel a connection that is special to you, one that is different from the connection I have with Reiki?

End here if you must. Next Meditation:

Level 1:

> Why should I be attuned to Level 2 and you?
>
> What will you add to MY Reiki?
>
> How will you help me be a better practitioner when doing Reiki on a client or myself?
>
> If I become attuned to Level 2, how will creating a personal relationship with you help me?

End here if you must. Next Meditation:

> What will you add to my healing sessions?
> What will you add to my life, not just in performing Reiki, but my life in general?
> What, if anything, is there about you that I should know now, especially in regard to continuing my Reiki training?

Levels 2 & 3:

> Is there anything about you that I am not aware of? If so, what?
> How can I use you in a healing session that is in complete harmony with who I am?
> How do you wish me to use you?

End here if you must. Next Meditation:

> Is there anything that I do now when invoking you that is not is in harmony with my higher self? If yes, what is it and how can I adjust that in order to be in harmony with my higher self?
> How can I create a personal relationship with you?
> How can I use you in my every day life?

When you are finished with each meditation, thank the symbol for allowing you to enter and slowly withdraw. Remember, you are still within the Reiki Energy. If you wish, if anything was brought up during your questioning of the symbol that you feel needs clarification, you can either ask the Reiki Energy now or meditate back at a later date. Thank the Reiki Energy before withdrawing from it.

If you are on Level 1, you can ask the questions I suggested for Level 2 & 3. It is my belief that Universe will not answer a question if we are not ready to receive the answer, so you lose nothing by asking. Levels 2 & 3, if your attention is drawn to a Level 1 question, by all means, ask. The answers you receive are your answers, and if you are lucky enough to be doing some of the mediations with another practitioner, in sharing your answers, you may be astounded by the various and different answers people receive. That is as it should be. There are no right or wrong answers when conversing with Universe. There are only your answers, which are true for you.

When you have finished this series of meditations you should be well on your way to having that private and personal knowledge that was given to you by Universe about each of Reiki's symbols. But what if, for whatever reason, you feel that those definitions are still not sufficient. What if, because of your life situation at the current time, you feel deep in your being, the symbols you have are not enough? What if you want more? What if you need more?

In the early years of 2000, I needed surgery to repair my left rotator cuff muscle. I lived alone at that time, and being a lefty, I knew I would have problems doing my regular daily activities. I already was a Reiki Master and I knew I would give myself Reiki. But I wanted something more than the four symbols. I wanted a wider door to open to let a specific part of Reiki Energy into me, a part that I knew I would need. What I wanted was a new symbol, a special symbol that would be specifically for the pain that I knew I would have.

I have told you that by doing these meditations generic Reiki would become your Reiki. I believed that then - I believe that now. A week before my operation, I meditated. Behind my closed eyes, I went to and saw the source of Reiki, just as you have done in the beginning of this book. I then called in Cho Ku Rei. From within both, being completely surrounded by the love, compassion, and understanding of Universe, I asked for a symbol. I knew that by invoking the Cho Ku Rei during my healing process, the intensity of Reiki Energy would increase. But I wanted a specific part of the Reiki Energy to increase. I wanted that part of Reiki that deals solely with pain to not only to enter me, but to be intensified when I combined it with the Cho Ku Rei. That's why I wanted to include both Reiki Energy and Cho Ku Rei in my meditation.

What I was given, or saw, or imagined (it didn't matter which) from within my meditation was something like this:

For me, this symbol made sense because it reminded me of the Celtic Tree of Life. The Tree connects the three realities in which all things exist. Its roots are securely planted in the lower world; its branches reach high into the upper world, and connecting the two, its trunk, the middle world, and the reality we live in. This is a shamanic concept of our three worlds, Upper, Middle, and Lower, and Lower does not refer to the Biblical concept of hell, but of a place where shamanic practitioners believe animal spirit guides dwell. The spiral line with its three loops wrapped around the tree only reinforced the rightness of this symbol because it reminded me of the connectedness not only between the three worlds, but our connectedness with each other and the world we live in.

I then asked for a name for this symbol and the words that came to me, in my own voice as I explained before were Roc Das.

It was there before me, Roc Das, this symbol that I asked

Universe for. I went to it and asked for permission to enter. I felt it's power - its warmth - its love. I remember tingles racing through my body just like the first time I entered the Reiki Energy. I breathed in as I asked you to do when you entered the Reiki Source. I swallowed and imagined Roc Das' energy going down into my stomach and spreading its power into every part of me. I felt its heat. At that moment I knew, I really knew, Reiki, Spirit, Universe had attuned me to this new symbol. I felt wonderful.

Reiki had given me a symbol, one that I needed to help me during my upcoming future. She had attuned me to it, just as she attuned Dr. Usui to his symbols. In the coming weeks, I used that symbol every night before I went to sleep and I believe that it helped me a great deal. Whether it did or did not was never an issue with me. Whether it was Roc Das that eased the pain, the effects of Reiki intensified by the Cho Ku Rei or simply a case of mind over matter, it didn't matter. What mattered was only what I believed in my heart. I believed that Roc Das was part of MY Reiki. My own true Reiki.

But wait! You are saying, how can I be so arrogant as to place myself on the same level as Dr. MIkao Usui. I'm not and I don't. Remember I told you that they are many different kinds of Reiki, and that each one has its own symbols? I Googled Karuna Reiki Symbols and was led to a web page that showed them. Lots of them. I never knew they were that many. Please, if you wish, do the same.

Look at all those symbols on that web page. Some of them are the same ones I use, others are different. I asked myself where did these symbols all come from? They didn't come from Dr. Usui. My answer was, from people, human beings, just like us. And how did these people find these symbols? I suggest the same way I did. They meditated to Reiki, the Universal Life Force, Spirit, The Divine Being, their higher self, their divine soul. The words I use to label where they meditated to or what they envisioned doesn't matter. They went to the same source that I did, to the same source that you do when you meditate. And that source answered them just like she answered us. The only difference is they asked a question that you have not thought of asking.

Aside from my own experience with Roc Das, how can I say that it works? I have only one example that I can share. I did though, in my classes and attunements that I carried out after finding Roc Das, attune my students to it. But I explained how and why I received the symbol and left its validity and use up to them.

Another thing that was happening at that time in my life was that I was assisting Llyn Roberts with her workshop in Shamanic Reiki. One of the participants mentioned that her husband had cancer. While on the phone to her, I explained about Roc Das, how I found it, how I believe I was attuned to it, and described the symbol to her. The next time we spoke she told me she took the symbol (I assume that she asked Universe to attune her to it) and used it on her husband. She said it helped more than just using the Cho Ku Rei alone. I would be a liar if I didn't say that made me feel great.

One of my biggest lessons in Reiki, in using her symbols, in knowing for myself the absolute truth that it is the practitioners' intention more than anything, more than the actual appearance of the symbols given to them by their Reiki Masters, happened later.

That participant sent everyone in the group an email, including me. In the email, she told them about Roc Das and how it helped her husband and offered it to the group. When I saw the image in the email, I smiled. I had not done a good job in describing to her the spiral wrapping around the trunk. I saved that drawing and pasted it below.

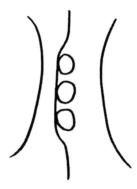

An obvious - it is not the same.

Another obvious - it didn't matter.

When she invoked it, it worked.

Why did it work? I believe that by her intention and keeping the idea of Roc Das within her mind and in her heart, when she asked Reiki to send the specific energy that I attributed to Roc Das to help alleviate some of her husband's pain, that plea was heard by Reiki. The compassionate nature of Reiki listened!

The implications to the above are monumental. This is one of the reasons why I love Reiki and why I wanted to share with you how you can make it your own. Not only did the symbol work for her, but also the symbol she used was different from the symbol I received. And it did not matter!

I'm going to pose some questions to you. It's not necessary to meditate to find the answers.

I believe it is only necessary for you to think about the questions.

I believe you will intuitively know the answers as soon as you read the questions.

If not now, you will discover for yourself those answers when you need them as you continue to walk the spiritual path. Just remember that the questions exist. You will find the answers, whether now or later, and when you do, you will know that the answers YOU found are just the answer YOU needed.

If you chose to meditate, please do. I do suggest that you only go to the Reiki Energy.

Is the purpose of a symbol just to focus the practitioner's intent and to make the practitioner concentrate on the energy and not on the shopping list? If no, what are their purposes?

Regardless of what symbols a Reiki Master attunes a person to, is it possible that after a Reiki I workshop, the participants have all the power they need to use all the symbols, but can't only because they either lack the knowledge that they exist or information about them?

Can you attune me to all the symbols?

Can I, when a need arises, ask and receive a symbol from you?

I did not include a break here because I believe, after reading what I suggested, you will know how to conduct your meditation so everything you need will be given to you at one time. I think this issue is so important that Universe will tell you everything you should know almost as soon as you ask. Also, if you meditate and receive a yes or no answer, follow up by asking for clarification.

Because there are so many symbols in the various types of Reiki (or other energy healing modalities for that matter), I do not believe that my experience is unique. I just believe that very few people have ever asked the question I did. I have explained why I believe the Universe would not give us a generic Reiki. The symbol I received is proof, at least for me, that Universe created for us a healing energy that can be fluid, depending on the situation.

I would think that at this point, (regardless if you have done the above meditation now) you must be asking yourself a series of questions dealing with some of the core tenets of Reiki. I know I asked myself questions after my initial meditation for a symbol, but I never meditated on them. I intuitively knew the answers as soon as I asked the questions. I didn't have to meditate because I was in complete harmony with the answers. I knew they were my answers. If you wish, I suggest at this point that you do either a first or second meditation to Reiki. I suggest you ask Reiki any questions that learning about Roc Das brought up for you. And if you would like, you can ask two of mine.

What does Reiki truly mean to me?
What is the extent or what are limits that you can personalize Reiki for me?

These questions and the ones that you ask may prove to be highly important. Also, if like me, you intuitively know the answers as soon as you have given voice to the questions, they ARE your answers, with or without meditating. The channel you have established with Reiki is becoming solid. If this has happened to you, you have learned another lesson. Intuition is one of the most important and understated aspects of Reiki.

Structure Vs. Intuition

Remember, the purpose of this book is to guide you as you find your way to claiming Reiki as your own. It is not meant to explain different Reiki philosophies and why people believe or reject those philosophies. I give you only the information I think is necessary for you to understand an issue so when you connect with the Reiki Energy as you have done before, you will be able to ask what position will deepen your connection to her in regard to that issue.

I said earlier, modern Reiki practitioners love to nit-pic. One of the major issues that they nit-pic about is the hand positions while performing Reiki. But hand positions are part of a more important issue dealing with Reiki structure in general and how practitioners deal with that structure. And there are only two choices. You follow the structure you were given or you allow yourself to be guided by your intuition.

In the following meditation, I will be asking you to begin to discover how you can best perform Reiki in a way that is in complete harmony with your higher self, with who you are.

For those of you who aren't aware, the issue of hand positions arises from a woman named Hawayo Takata. In 1935, she went to Japan and being ill, found out about a Reiki clinic/school. She had many Reiki sessions, was cured of her illness. Of course, she was sold on the healing modality. She was attuned to Levels 1 & 2 in Japan and then returned to the Hawaii. In 1938 one of her teachers from Japan visited her and attuned her to Level 3. Mrs. Takata became the first Reiki Master in the United States. In her lifetime, she attuned twenty-two Reiki Masters, and much of all Western Reiki is a result of her teachings of those twenty-two Masters, and they in turn, teaching many others.

Mrs. Takata standardized twelve hand positions for giving Reiki. She taught those positions to her students and her students taught them to their students. Even though Reiki Energy goes where it is needed in the body, Mrs. Takata felt that having a set structure for these hand positions was very important. To me, it seems trivial. To many, it is not. To some, if you don't do Reiki the way Mrs. Takata taught it, you aren't doing Reiki.

In a typical Reiki session, (as done by practitioners who follow Mrs. Takata's guidelines) the practitioner will begin standing behind the client's head. Beginning with the first hand position, the practitioner keeps his/her hands in that position for three to four minutes. Then a slow process begins, moving the hands from position to position, slowly down the client's body. The order usually is: head, neck, shoulders, chest, stomach, calves, legs, and feet. Some practitioners (myself included) then ask the client to turn over, and the practitioner moves back towards the head, but at a faster pace than going down. The whole session lasts between 45 to 60 minutes. Also, (and as mentioned in How Do You Perform Reiki) many practitioners keep their hands slightly above the client's body with the exception of the head and neck. Others place their hands lightly on the client. Both of these are also issues. Some believe that you need to follow Mrs. Takata's teaching - others don't.

Though the issue is hand positions, the greater issue for you is how should you perform Reiki in a way that is in harmony with who you are? I don't want to get involved in the discussions about the different ways of holding a session with a client. I want you to discover that on your own. My way is unimportant. I want you to find after meditating with Universe your own center. What is the best way to empower yourself to become the best practitioner you can? If hand positions work for you, then use them. If they don't, follow your intuition. Remember, there is no right or wrong way to do Reiki. There is only doing Reiki.

Begin this meditation as you have the others. The only difference now is which part of Reiki you will seek. If you discovered that any one of symbols you spoke to touched you in your heart and emotional self more than the others, more than the total Reiki Energy, then you may wish to go directly to that symbol. In that case, you don't need to visualize yourself entering the Reiki Energy. Visualize your (and it is now becoming YOUR) symbol directly. You should remember though that the totality of the Reiki Energy is always available and close by and you can move from symbol to the all encompassing Reiki Energy within your visualized mediation any time you wish.

If you are on Level 1, you too can meditate to either the Reiki Energy as you did in the first meditation, or, if you established the beginnings of a relationship with a symbol, even though you have not been attuned to it, you too may go directly to that symbol. Why do I say you can do this? Simple - I have complete trust in Universe. If the symbol did not wish to communicate with you on a deeper level than you did in your first meditation to it, it wouldn't have made a deeper connection with you. If you wish an affirmation of this, in your meditation, visual first the Reiki Energy. From there, ask it whatever concerns you have about going directly to a symbol you really don't know much about except what you read on the Internet. (Of course, I remind you that you meditated and asked Reiki, "Can you attune me to all the symbols?")

Up until now you have done several meditations to the Reiki Energy and should have a much deeper understanding and connection with Universal Life Force. Though it is always up to you, I again suggest that the meditation below should not be done in one sitting, but may require several sessions. In these meditations, you will ask questions directly related to what YOU DO in a Reiki session. The answers will show you YOUR Reiki, as Reiki feels you should practice it.

These are my suggested questions for your meditation. You can supply your own.

What is the best way for me to channel Reiki Energy?
What, in all I learned, is most important for me to remember? Why?
What, in all I learned, is least important for me to remember? Why?
There is a structure (hands on or above/hand positions/general procedures for a Reiki session, or any other procedures you were taught) built into Reiki. Is that structure in harmony with my higher self? If not, how can I perform those tasks and be in harmony with my higher self?

End here if you must. Next Meditation:

Is there a belief that I have but must I give up or alter in some way in order to become more harmonious with Reiki, with the Universal Life Force. If yes, what is that belief?

(Also if yes.) Will you show me that I may experience within my meditation, what my Reiki sessions (add if you wish - and my life in general) will look like with that altered that belief? (Also if yes.) Will you show me the first three steps I must take in order to give up or alter that belief?

Add-Ons

An issue that you will eventually have to deal with, if you have not dealt with it before, is called an add-on. Add-ons are the umbrella title for anything that a person includes in their Reiki session that was not taught by either Dr. Usui or Mrs. Takata. I mention them so you can put them into your basket of knowledge to see what if anything resonates within you, would empower you and help complete your foundation so you can fully claim Reiki as your own. For me, it is the add-ons that fully empowered me.

By now, the Reiki you know could be anywhere from the same as before you started reading to something vastly different, something much more personal. Or it could lie anywhere along a continuum with each possibility above on either end.

Just as I found some of the aspects of Reiki not in complete harmony with myself, others, who have come before me, have also found the same and have widened the scope of a Reiki session to include procedures that are not from Dr. Usui's Reiki. Most are not even from Reiki. This movement away from the traditional Usui Reiki I, described in the beginning of this text, is now being widely discussed. Many practitioners are in favor of them - many are opposed, and the discussions can be very lively, with each side being adamant in their opinion.

Crystals are an example. Dr. Usui did not use crystals in his Reiki. I mentioned earlier that I was interested in crystal healing energy. On many occasions, I slipped a crystal into my clients' hand and asked them to do a simple visualization to help in their own healing. That is an example of an add-on.

For me, whether add-ons should or should not be used is not an issue. The issue should be not IF the practitioner uses an add-on, but WHY the practitioner uses an add-on? And the answer goes to the heart of this book. I believe that practitioners who use add-ons, and I include myself, do so because they feel that something within the scope of traditional Reiki is lacking. It is that sense of empowerment I want you to feel deep in your very being. When practitioners use their knowledge and their expertise, gained in other healing modalities to enhance the total healing effect of the Reiki session, how can that be misusing the Universal gift we all have received? You cannot do Reiki wrong. Once you connect with the Reiki Energy (done by simply calling out to Universe that you are ready to begin to channel Reiki) the Energy flows. Period. A practitioner cannot channel Reiki incorrectly. The Energy would not allow it.

If the practitioner adds something to the Reiki session that he/she believes will increase the overall healing effect for their clients (and empowering themselves at the same time), why should others who don't accept add-ons object? I believe that Reiki's ultimate goal is to bring a sense of peace, a healing harmony and balance into our world. I do not think that Reiki objects to using its healing energy in harmony with the energy given off by a crystal. And who is to say that crystal energy is not an aspect of Reiki Energy? Crystals are born within Mother Earth. Crystals are part of Universe. And if crystals are not part of Reiki, surely they are a very close relative! However, to remain within a state of honesty and integrity, practitioners must let their clients know in the beginning of the session that they may or will use a healing technique that is not part of the traditional Usui Reiki system. This may require a discussion, depending on the add-on.

There are many different types of add-ons, but since the nature of this text is to bring you closer to achieving a personal relationship with the Energy, I only will discuss the ones I believe will increase your relationship with the Reiki Energy.

Add-On
Reiki Guides

Those familiar with Reiki know that Reiki is not a religion. You do not have to have any set belief system before being attuned to Reiki and there are no religious beliefs you must accept after being attuned. Being asked to follow set procedures in performing Reiki is not in any way religious. On the contrary, Reiki will fit into any religious system. If you are a Christian, Jew, Muslim, Hindu, or part of any other religious or Spiritual group, Reiki is compatible with that belief system.

Yet, I have known, have spoken to or worked with, people who have religious beliefs and wish to incorporate those beliefs into their Reiki practice. When students of mine have asked if that is possible, I tell them yes and explain it this way.

If a person prays to Deity as part of their religious belief system, then they already have a personal relationship with Deity and meditate (pray) to him/her in order to seek guidance or ask that figure to help them overcome a present problem. What can be more empowering than to have a private conversation with Deity, and come away with knowing that Deity has listened to the prayer? That doesn't mean that prayers will be answered immediately or even that they will be granted. It just means that the person seeking Divine aid knows that he/she was listened to and that whatever will be done, will be done with the knowledge and approval of Deity, even if the outcome is not what they desire.

I know I have over simplified this tremendously, but I do so in order to keep this as simple as I can. Some Reiki practitioners feel more comfortable knowing that when they practice Reiki, they do so with the knowledge, approval and help of a Reiki Guide. That guide can be part of their religious belief system or it can be anything or anyone.

Several former students, wishing to incorporate Reiki within their personal beliefs, actively chose Jesus as their guide. Jesus was one of the greatest healers in history so invoking His name and bringing His energy into a healing session seems a natural extension of Universal Life Force Energy. Some may chose a Saint or religious prophet to work with them during a Reiki session. Who they name to help during a Reiki session doesn't matter. By holding the thought of their religious figure in their heart and mind, the Reiki practitioner is empowered because of the personal relationship the practitioner has with that figure.

Other practitioners choose to meditate for the purpose of finding a guide. They may find an ancestor, either a direct one or a tribal one from the far past. They may find someone else. In some spiritual practices, such as shamanism, guides can be in the form of animals or objects of nature. It doesn't matter what form the guide takes. What does matter is that those practitioners who have Reiki guides know that their guides are not in the same reality we live in, but in the same reality as the Reiki Energy. Some practitioners find it is easier to communicate with a guide than the Reiki Energy during a session. For those, guides can be a great help.

Practitioners who use guides usually visualized their guide in the beginning of a session and know in their heart, that their guide is going to be with them during the session. Reiki will not mind.

What I'd like to suggest now is that you meditate and connect with your Reiki Guide.

I should have said this earlier but since I have not, I say it now. If, after reading what I suggest you do in the meditation process, you feel that the entire meditation is not for you, then don't do it. If you can think of a way to do what I suggest that is in harmony with your higher self, then do that. And if not, just move on to the next section. Remember, the point of this book is to empower you to do your Reiki in the best possible way that is in harmony with who you are. If Reiki guides holds no interest for you, then Reiki guides hold no interest for you. That being said, this is what I suggest you do.

As before, meditate to the source of Reiki. My suggestion is to enter the Reiki light first and then, if you so desire, call on your symbol and enter that. From that space, hugged within the love, understanding and compassion of Reiki Energy, ask your Reiki guide to enter the light or ask the Universal Life Force to take you to your Reiki Guide.

Don't prejudge this meditation. Don't expect anyone, anything, any force of nature. Just ask and give yourself permission to accept what the Reiki Energy will show you. These are the questions I suggest when your guide appears.

Why are you my Reiki guide?
You are part of Reiki and can appear before me in any form. Why have you chosen this form?
What is happening in my life that has made you come to me now?
What lessons do you hope to teach me?

End here if you must. Next Meditation:

What will you add to MY Reiki?
How can you help me in deepening my connection with Reiki?
When I call on you during a Reiki session, what kind of help or guidance can I expect?
What do I need to know about you?

Should you decide to do this (these) meditation(s), I'm sure the answers you receive will be enough to begin a relationship with your guide. In case you are a bit hesitant in attempting to find a guide, allow me to share this with you. It may help you decide.

Many years ago, before I began to teach Reiki, I attended a workshop given by John Matthews. John is a widely known and respected shamanic teacher who is based in England. What I remember most about that workshop was it furthered my belief that Universe could and would react to each of us on a very personal level. We usually think we know what is best for us. But many times we don't. Universe, on the other hand, always knows and acts accordingly.

This occurred during a discussion John had with us when he referred to his spirit guide. I apologize to John and you for not being able to state with any certainty that what I say John said was in reality what John actually did say. But I am certain he said something like it and that is enough to make my point.

John's guide was a man whose history is shrouded in unknowns. An early medieval Welsh poet who lived in the 6th century, a bard, a singer of songs, a shaman of extraordinary wisdom, who some believe was one of the magical Druids. His name was Taliesin.

But that's not important. What is important is that John said when he meditated to Taliesin, he always appeared wearing a cloak and his head was hidden within the folds of a hood. John told us that he once asked Taliesin why he appeared before him like that. At that point, Taliesin removed his cloak. John said he saw a great light coming from the place where Taliesin had stood. And John heard, in his voice, just like you have heard the answers to your questions in your voice, Taliesin's answer. "I am energy. Had I appeared to you in this form the first time, you would not have known how to relate to me." John agreed.

For us, the relevance of Taliesin's answer to John is this. Your Reiki guide is part of Reiki - within the circle that is Reiki, just as the symbols are inside the circle that is Reiki. To many, Reiki is an abstract concept. She is light. She is energy. She is a Universal Life Force. For some, it is difficult to connect with an abstract form. (That's what I think Taliesin meant when he said John would not have been able to relate to him as pure energy.) Your Reiki guide is in a concrete form, one that is much easier to communicate with because its form is far more familiar to you than the abstract form of Reiki. Whatever guide you find, that guide is light, that guide is the Universal Life Force Energy, dwelling in the same reality as Reiki, part of but different, like the symbols, but appearing to you in a form that is more compatible within our reality.

In other words, your Reiki guide is Reiki, coming to you in the way she knows will be the easiest for you to relate to, and deepen your relationship with her. The two, Reiki and Guide, are the same, merged together yet separate to make your gift truly personal.

For your consideration, this idea, I offer.

Add-On
Scanning

Up until now, I have avoided telling you what I do in my sessions with clients. What works for me may not work for you. What personal beliefs I have regarding Reiki may or may not be compatible with your beliefs. This book is not about me teaching you what to do. It is about you, after meditating with Reiki, teaching yourself what to do. Not only must you pay the price, trust and believe, but you must know deep within your very being that what you do when performing Reiki is what you must do. And the wonderful thing about paying the price is that you do not need anyone's permission to do what you do.

In this section, I want to explain something I do in my sessions because in the beginning of my Reiki career, it helped me a great deal in trusting my intuition, and that, I believe was very important in empowering me. That thing is scanning.

Early on, you read that I was interested in energy healing, not just in Reiki but also in other modalities. In my search for information, I attended a workshop in "TT" or Therapeutic Touch. All I want to say about Therapeutic Touch is the following:

It was developed by two women, Dolores Krieger, Ph.D., R.N., and her teacher, Dora Kunz, who was a "natural" healer. "TT" is an energy therapy that practitioners believe will promote healing to reduce pain and anxiety. In Therapeutic Touch, the practitioners place their hands on or near a patient. They feel their client's energy and then alter it for their patient's benefit.

If you wish to learn more about "TT", just Google it, and you will find more information than you can possible digest in a reasonable time.

One workshop does not an expert make. And that is all I attended. But I was intrigued by the knowledge that by scanning a client's body, the practitioner could feel their energy. If they sensed that energy from a particular area, the leg for instance, was not in harmony with the rest of client's body, they altered it. Though I was able to do that in the workshop, I wasn't comfortable with altering another person's energy, especially using my own energy to do it. I wondered if I could apply that method with Reiki because I knew that if I could, it would be the Reiki Energy that would change a client's energy field, not mine. And because of my complete trust in Reiki never to harm and only do what is the best interest of the person, I felt 100% at ease using the technique in my sessions. Later I found out that not only could you do it with Reiki, but also some Reiki Masters teach it in their workshops. Eventually, I did too.

The "how" I do it is simple. Usually, after I finished applying Reiki on the front of a client, but before I ask him/her to turn over, I moved my open hands, palm down, slowly over the client's body. Before I started, I shook my hands in the air, wiped them on my shirt, and shook them again. I wanted to remove any feeling I had of the Reiki Energy flowing through my hands. Then I began moving them.

I concentrated not on my client's energy or even the Reiki Energy, but on my hands. As I moved them over the body, I was looking for a difference in the way my hands felt. When I started, my hands felt neutral - nothing special. But then, as I passed them over a part of the body, I felt something, heat or a tingling sensation. Others I have spoken to also felt heat, but sometimes coolness or an itch. What it IS doesn't matter. The fact that it "IS" something does.

Whenever I felt that feeling, I stopped, placed my hands gently on the client and called on the Reiki Energy to flow into him/her at that point. I left my hands there for a moment. Then, I continued scanning the body. Whenever I felt something different in my hands, I repeated the process.

I have just made a major contradiction because I have stated that Reiki Energy goes wherever it is needed and the practitioner has no idea where that is. This is still true. So how can I say scanning is empowering?

For me, it makes no difference whether or not I was taking an active part in helping the Reiki Energy decide where to go. But the issue is not whether or not I was taking an active part.

The issue is, did I believe I was. Yes, I did.

And sometimes, not all the time, a client would ask me after the session was over why did I return and put my hands on his knee or arm or calf again at one point? When I asked why he/she had asked, the client would tell me about an ache or pain, new or old, they had in that part of the body and it felt better now.

Did I do anything? No.

Did I heal that person, if only for a little while? No. Reiki did.

But did I FEEL like I helped. Absolutely.

Reiki Masters often say in their workshops, "When ego goes, Reiki flows." Reiki should be an ego-less modality. I said in the beginning that we, as practitioners, do not do anything once the

Reiki Energy enters us before entering the client. That is a major asset about Reiki. It works regardless of what we do. But I contend it is also what is wrong with Reiki because it doesn't empower me to know that I do nothing!

It doesn't help me to know that I have done, am doing, and will do absolutely nothing when it comes to performing Reiki.

If Reiki does all of the work and all the healing, then what's left for me or us to do? Nothing!

But we are all human beings and having an ego is part of us. How can we reconcile the fact that we know we don't do anything and yet we need to know we that we are doing something?

The answer is, for me, taking a leap of faith. I may be wrong, but I don't think that there are too many religious scholars today who will say that Mother Earth is only five or six thousand years old. If you applied a strict interpretation to the Bible, I think that's approximately what you would come up with. I don't wish to open a Pandora's box containing all the issues how science and religion conflict with each other. My point for mentioning it is that I believe most religious individuals can separate religious doctrine from scientific doctrine. Religion is not science. It is accepting something purely on faith. Science is not religion. It is accepting something purely on facts or overwhelming evidence of facts. The two, religion and science, can exist side by side even if they have opposing views on a given topic. Dinosaurs lived on the earth millions of years ago, not thousands. But that shouldn't and doesn't stop a religious person from believing in the Bible. Religion is because Religion is. Period. That sounds just like something I said very early in this text. Reiki is Reiki. It exists. So what does that have to do with scanning?

I need to know that I am doing more than nothing.

I need to know I am someone who has a worth when it comes to performing Reiki.

Why is it that there are so many people whom never go

beyond Level 1 in Reiki? In my career as a Reiki Master Teacher, I have attuned far more people to Reiki I than Reiki II? I touched on this issue when I asked the Reiki I practitioners to look up the symbols and meditate to them. Is it possible that some people (not only Level 1 practitioners) who do not feel empowered by Reiki eventually stop using it? I don't know - I can't answer that. But I can say this.

This book is about knowing in your heart, in your head, in your being that you have a worth when it comes to channeling Reiki Energy.

You, just as I, want to have a say in it, a say in what we do and a say in how we do it. I believe that is why you are reading this book. That's why I have suggested all the meditations within so you can find out what your say is by asking the source.

I accept the truth of Reiki without question.

I accept that what I do and feel is an important part of Reiki.

I choose NOT to let the issue of where the energy goes be in conflict because I believe when I ask of Reiki, and the reason is valid, Reiki will listen.

When I scan clients, I accept on faith, that where I place my hands after following my intuition will affect the flow of energy. Reiki will cure/heal or not on its own and I have no say in that.

But when my intention, when my concern for my client is such that I ask the Reiki Energy to please enter the body in this place, to please stay in this place, and please bring additional healing to this place, Reiki will listen.

I have mentioned before the three qualities Universe has: love, understanding, and compassion. Reiki, Universal Life Force Energy, pours those attributes out to us and the us is not just the client. The us includes you and I as practitioners.

Reiki will listen because in her wisdom, she knows what the ego is.

Reiki will listen because she knows that we cannot continue acting as her agent and feeling that we are not part of the process.

Reiki will listen because she wants her gift to be spread to as many people as possible, and she knows that when people do not feel they are part of the process, they may stop being part of the process.

For me, the two are not on opposite ends of a spectrum. Universal Life Force Energy, Reiki, goes where it needs to go and we do not know where that is.

Universal Life Force Energy, Reiki, will go where I ask it to go when I scan my clients. In accepting both, I empower myself. I offer that for your consideration.

I do not ask you to accept what you have just read simply because I have written it. I believe it is important, but what works for me doesn't have to work for you.

I suggest you think about what you have just read and then do a simple meditation to Reiki Energy or your symbol. I would ask the following:

How is it possible to have two opposite beliefs when performing Reiki without those beliefs being in conflict?

If that question doesn't sound right to you, ask whatever you need to. You need to find your own answers as you continue your journey to empowering yourself. Remember, the answer will be yours. Even if you don't meditate on this issue, but as soon as you read the question I posed, you knew intuitively the answer, that answer is still your answer. It is still correct.

Add-On
Crystals and Stones

Earlier in the text I mentioned that I was attracted to crystal healing. I purchased the book, "Crystal Co-Creators" by Dorothy Reoder, which I highly recommend. I raised the topic in connection to my beginning to learn that how I felt about something was often more important than what I read or was told about that same thing. Now, I mention it in the context of an add-on.

Crystals give off energy and many people can feel that energy. I won't go into listing the various crystals or their qualities, there are far to many crystals with far to many attributes to cover here. Besides, I don't claim to be an expert in crystals. I just use them. And if what I say now resonates with you, I believe you can use them without buying a book or knowing what others say they do for humanity. You are humanity. You can decide for yourself.

The first crystal I bought was a small rose quartz ball. When I touched it for the first time, I felt a soft, gentle, warming energy. At the time, I was too dense, too ensconced in the idea that I had to accept what others dictated before Aimee scolded me for not trusting myself, to realize that I missed a major teaching, listening to my inner voice first. It took me a long time to figure that out.

The book says rose quartz works on your heart. It helps if you are sad or depressed. It helps you to find inner peace. It helps make you whole. No wonder I was drawn to it because at the time, my personal life was in complete disarray. Even today, I never leave the house without putting that same small rose quartz ball in my pocket.

I cannot write in this section all you need to do to be in harmony with crystals. If you don't know anything about them and are feel that you need some knowledge before striking out on your own, you might like to purchase Ms. Reoder's book. Here, I will just tell you what I think you can do to use crystals or other stones successfully in a Reiki session safely.

Finding crystals or stones are very easy if you trust yourself. I say stones because many of the people I met in various workshops had small collections of stones, pebbles and/or crystals that they used in their healings. If you are walking in a park or woods, and your eyes, for no particular reason, rest on a stone, I suggest you go to it and pick it up. You can if you wish use the same technique I used in scanning and see how your hands feel when you pick it up. Concentrate on the feelings in your hand, not the stone, as you pick it up. If you notice a difference, take the stone. Or do a very quick waking meditation - ask the stone if it wishes to come with you. The answer should come right away. If no, put it back where you found it. If yes, take it. Do the same in a crystal shop. Crystal shops usually have smaller crystals at a very reasonable cost. You don't need to buy large shiny expensive crystals - you need to buy ones that are waiting for you.

Crystals and stones are really the same, aren't they? They both come from Mother Earth. They both have a deep connection to the Earth; they are both one of the four basic elements.

You need to "clear" them when you get home. Soak the stones or crystals in salt water. Sea salt is best, if not, either kosher salt or just table salt. I let them soak for an hour or so. If you have a glass bowl, use that. If not, not. Once removed and dried, if you can, put them on a windowsill and let them stay in the sun all day. Or put them on the soil of a plant (or in a garden if you have one). What you want to do is clear stone/crystal of its past energy (and yes, the stone has energy too). Both sunlight and being on soil can do that. After clearing them, hold each in your hand and "charge or program" them with your intention. I now suggest you do a meditation. With the stone or crystal in your hand (do one at a time) meditate to the stone or crystal itself. Just imagine it. You can enter it if you wish or just keep the image in front of you. You only have one question to ask.

How do you wish me to use you in my Reiki practice?

The crystal or stone has already told you that it wanted to go with you. Trust that it knew why you wanted it. You do not have to ask if it will help you, you only have to ask it how it will help you. When you have finished the meditation, before putting the stone or crystal down, charge it, program it with your energy, your thoughts, your intentions. You could say something like, "I ask you to use your energy in the best interest of my clients and help bring about the healing that is needed." Or you could say, "I charge you with removing negative energy from this house or from my clients and send that energy back to the Universal Energy, to be transformed and returned to earth for the purpose of doing good." In essence, you are telling the crystal or stone what specific task you would like it to perform. This task should be in harmony with the information you retrieved in your meditation.

Using crystals is not difficult. I say that because I used them in the most general of ways. I always tried to do the simplest thing when applying any add-on to Reiki.

Whenever I had a Reiki session, on a small table next to the massage table, I had several crystals and/or stones. I selected them in the same way I scanned. I moved my hands over my collection while holding the intention, "Who wants to help during the healing?" I always got an answer.

Then, during the session, if I felt an energy blockage and after scanning the blockage was still there, or if my mind just wandered towards that table and a specific crystal on it while I was doing Reiki, I picked the crystal up and either placed it on the client or put it in their hand. I used my intuition to help me decide as opposed to doing a quick meditation. I would ask the clients, by using their imagination, to visualize the energy blockage I felt or if they sensed anything within themselves that they intuitively knew was not in their higher good, to imagine whatever it was being drawn into the crystal. If the crystal was in their hand, I would gently guide the blocked energy or what the client wanted removed up their body, down into the arm and then their hand. When the client told me what we were moving was within the crystal, I took it from them and dropped it into a bowl of salt water also on the little table. If I placed the crystal on then, I asked them to imagine the crystal being a magnet, drawing into it anything they wanted to rid themselves of. Again, when they said that what that to be moved was within the crystal, I removed it. I never, not even the first time I used crystals, had a negative feedback from a client saying he/she felt that the crystal did not help. (But, to refer back to something I said, in talking to clients before the session, they were aware that I use crystals and were comfortable with it.)

Crystals have a place in energy healing. They can help draw out negative energy - they can help put in positive energy. The same goes for your stones. I have told you one of the ways that I use them but following the purpose of this text, I want you to empower yourself. You need to find your own answer. When you asked the crystal or stone in your meditation how do you wish me to use you, you should have gotten the answer. If not, meditate to Reiki Energy itself and ask the same question.

Does it make a difference?

No.

Why? Remember when I suggested that your Reiki Guide could be a manifestation of Reiki, Universal Life Force Energy but in a form easier to relate to? The answer is similar. Reiki is part of Universe as is our own Mother Earth. Crystals, and of course, stones, are part of Mother Earth, and therefore, they are part of the Energy, part of Reiki. Reiki knows the same answers as the crystals, so go to whichever you feel more comfortable with and find the answer designed for you. The longer you travel the path we are on, the more times you realize that everything on that path, regardless of modality, is connected in some way.

Two last items and they are important. When I finished using the crystal (or stone) I dropped it into the salt water. If you have a second client coming in, do not use the same crystal. They must be cleared of your clients' energy. Repeat the same procedure I outlined above for clearing the crystal or stone after each use.

Also, if you live in house, or a place where you can easily go outside and do the following, please do so. Instead of pouring the salt water from the bowl down the drain, go outside and pour it on the ground. The reason is you wish the energy drawn from the client and now in the water to go back to Mother Earth. If you feel inclined to do so, as you pour it out, hold the intent of asking Mother Earth to transmute the energy and return it to the Universal Energy flow. Don't pour the water out in the same place every time. The salt is no good for the plants. But the small amount of salt you use should not harm anything. Washing out the bowl with just soap and water is fine.

Add-On
Time Release Reiki

I have said that the Universal Energy will take into account, based on our intent and purpose, our wishes. In the beginning of the section on scanning, I told you it is not my intention to tell you what to do, but rather, after you meditate to the source, you should know yourself what to do. What you eventually decide on is going to be your Reiki, and your decision will be based on your experiences during your meditations. I think I can say that Reiki, Universal Life Force Energy, is therefore, in reality, your teacher. I hope you accept this because I wish to state the following cliché:

When the student is ready, the teacher will appear.

When I was ready, I went to my teacher (Hon Sha Ze Sho Nen) and asked why I was not happy with what I was doing.

When I was ready, I went to my teacher (Reiki) and asked for a symbol.

I now offer a new concept for your consideration for knowing when you are ready.

When the question within you arises, when life presents you with situation that you think Reiki could be of help and existing Reiki is not sufficient, ask your question. It will be answered.

If I meditated to Reiki and asked for a few new symbols because I wanted to establish a new and different kind of Reiki in order to fill my living room with new (and paying) students, I don't know if Reiki would have answered as she did in the past. I hope she wouldn't. I have said many times that your intention is one of the most important facets of Reiki. Reiki knows why questions are being asked and I believe that if the questions are not asked from within in a circle of honor, integrity and impeccability, you will not receive an answer. This leads me to the topic of Time Release Reiki.

I was attuned to Reiki II and Reiki III by a student of William Rand, who is the founder of "The International Center for Reiki Training" (http://www.reiki.org.) I use his workbooks for my workshops and his website is a wonderful source of information. He also publishes a Newsletter. In 2002, I read an article called "Time Released Reiki" by Bonnie Bercume which you can find by going to William's website, clicking on "Reiki Articles" and from there, clicking on "160 More Articles." The article states that in mediation, Bonnie received a new way of using the Hon Sha Ze Sho Nen, a new way of using Reiki.

I put the following in the form of a hypothetical because I do not know why Bonnie meditated asking for that new way of using Reiki, and the article on William's website does not mention it. For the purpose of this book, the why is not relevant because it is my belief that the reason Bonnie asked was important enough for Reiki to answer.

Imagine Bonnie had a client, child or grandchild, and wanted to send Reiki Energy to that person very often. But that would be impractical. It would mean she, or any practitioner, would have spend hours sending Reiki. After meditating to Reiki, Bonnie shared the answer with the Reiki world.

She, by her intention, asked Reiki, asked Hon Sha Ze Sho Nen, to create a sphere of Reiki Energy over the person she wanted to send Reiki to. She then asked Reiki, that once an hour for a period twenty-four hours, to release and send to the person, just the right amount of energy that he/she needed at that moment.

Rather simple, isn't it. And it's not in any books that I am aware of. I know it wasn't taught by Dr. Usui' Reiki or Mrs. Takata's. But Bonnie claimed in the article that she used it and found it effective. I assume she didn't get bogged down in discussions about what you can and can't do in Reiki. I assume she didn't wait for approval from her teacher or from other Reiki practitioners. Bonnie went to the source and asked. The answer she received resonated within her. She knew in her heart it was correct. Her response may have been, "I like that. It makes sense to me. I'm going to try it." She did and it worked, and in doing so, Bonnie not only claimed her Reiki, but she added for all to use, a new technique in Reiki's arsenal.

I tried Time Release Reiki, but didn't do it often, and eventually, I stopped. The reason was it didn't empower me. I found that after sending the Reiki Energy and getting on with my daily mundane activities, I forgot about it. It didn't make me feel that I was part of anything. That was the same reason why I went to Hon Sha Ze Sho Nen and found how I could use it in a way that was in harmony with myself. I have said several times, what works for me may not work for you. Well, what worked for Bonnie didn't work for me. But this does not lessen in any way the effectiveness of Time Release Reiki, just as it doesn't lessen the effect of anything I have said that doesn't resonate with you. But in conducting my Reiki classes after reading the article and trying it myself, I always explained the technique and left it up to them to decide if they wished to put it into their basket of knowledge in dealing with how to perform Reiki. Information cannot hurt. Unfortunately, I never received any feedback regarding Time Release Reiki from my students.

By now, some of you may be wondering about a central issue this text may bring up. You may have glimpsed the issue when I told you about Roc Das or when I asked you to meditate on the question, "What is the extent or what are limits that you can personalize Reiki for me?" This issue was brought up by my publisher on his first reading of a very early and poorly edited submission of my proposal.

Though it was in a slightly different context, he wondered, "How far you can expand the 'shape' of Reiki before it loses any definition?

The wonderful thing about this question is I don't have to answer it for you. I'm not the teacher, remember? But I know my answer and am happy to share it with you. However, you need to begin to form your own answer. Mine is the following:

I believe that Reiki is bounded and contained only by the limits of our imagination. I believe that the shapes of Reiki are infinite. I believe that instead of Reiki defining herself and expecting us to mold ourselves around that definition, Reiki molds herself around us, around our higher good, around our intention. She does not define herself. She allows us to define her and then accepts our definition.

That's why Reiki can mean different things to different people. That means strict traditional Reiki practitioners find exactly the same love, understanding and compassion as I do, a very nontraditional practitioner. We both have a deep belief in Reiki and can go to her whenever we need to. We are both correct in our belief systems and Reiki listens to and answers both of us. Problems only occur when people do not accept the equality of both kinds of practitioners. I choose not to get involved with the issue of who is right or wrong because I don't need, and neither do you, any validation other than our own personal one, in how we practice Reiki. Besides, you can't do Reiki wrong!

Are there procedures that Reiki would not do for me?

Are there definitions that I may give to Reiki that she will not accept?

I answered both before. Yes.

Why? If my intent, if my purpose is not for the higher good of my client, or will not benefit Reiki in general, then Reiki will have no part in it. Of that I am certain. Bonnie asked Reiki for help - Reiki answered. In finding Roc Das, I asked Reiki for help - Reiki answered. Both fit the above criteria. Can you do that? Of course you can. Imagine a Level 1 practitioner (not knowing that symbols even exist in Reiki) after seeing the effects of a forest fire, going to the window, holding his/her arms up, and sending Reiki to the forest to help heal it and aid in its re-growth. Do you think Reiki would say, "I'd love to help, but without the Hon Sha Ze Sho Nen, there is nothing I can do." Of course not. Do you think you could you stop reading this book now and continue on your own? Of course. (Oops!)

You have another meditation. I suggest you go to the Reiki Energy and ask her the following questions. Mine or yours. Whatever is in your heart.

What is your true definition?

What are your limits?

What are the edges of your boundaries?

Add-On
Aromatherapy

Though I'm sure you are aware of Aromatherapy, let me define it in its simplest terms. Its is a form of complementary healing that uses essential oils (made from plants or plant parts), in order to help promote healing.

Again, like with Therapeutic Touch, I attended a workshop in beginning aromatherapy. And again, I was intrigued by the modality. But I realized very early on that to use aromatherapy properly, you need to put in the time, the energy, the effort and the study. There are many oils, and each one has it's own properties and is used for healing a different aspect of the client. Many of those healing properties overlap and to use aromatherapy effectively, you have to know what each oil does. Also, if several oils help with the same condition, the aromatherapist should have specific reason for selecting one oil over the other. I had none of the above knowledge.

My interest was in Reiki and how I could enhance it by incorporating aspects of other modalities. Unlike "TT" where the little knowledge I had could easily fit into a Reiki session, I couldn't do that with aromatherapy. There was too much I didn't know and I wasn't willing to put in the effort to learn it. I wanted to put my efforts into Reiki. But I liked the effect the various oils had on me and if there was a way, I would use it.

I knew that the experts in the field of aromatherapy, the teacher I had as well as the authors of the books I used, all attributed the same healing properties to the same oils. I accepted their expertise. What they said the oils did, they did. I knew I would not use the oils directly on a client because I didn't feel comfortable with that (not knowing what I was doing) but I would use a diffuser and put the aroma of the oil into the air. That could do no harm. One of things I did learn was that the essential oil, lavender, was considered one of the most important oils and is a must have oil in any aromatherapist's supply closet. One of its properties is that it helps in relaxation.

I wanted to use that oil to help relax the students in my workshops or my Reiki clients. I wanted to help them get rid of any anxieties they may have about Reiki, the class or session, and open them up to the possibilities Reiki may hold for them.

I said earlier that when a practitioner uses an add-on, they should let their clients know. I admit I didn't do that with the oil. It was there on the table when they arrived, a tea light candle under a ceramic half bowl filled with water and several drops of lavender oil. When anyone asked, I explained what it was and why it was there. If it bothered someone, I removed it. Where Reiki is fueled by intentions, aromatherapy isn't. At least, I don't think it is. Where my Reiki is filled with empowerment, aromatherapy did not hold any empowerment for me. The oil does the works and the empowerment comes from the practitioner's knowledge in selecting the proper oil. I never had that knowledge. But I used it anyway. I picked the one aspect of aromatherapy, the one oil I knew I could use safely and used it. I told myself that as a bonus, lavender could also help heal in ways other than relaxing. Even though I had no idea what those ways were, I figured it couldn't hurt. Lavender did what lavender did. Did it help? I didn't, and still don't know. Then why did I continue to use it?

I need to explain a little about myself in order to answer that question. In 1995, my wife died very suddenly of an aorta aneurysm while we were in Vienna visiting relatives. Several months later, I began walking the path I am still on. To be honest, when I began my healing work, it wasn't for the benefit of others; it was to find healing for myself, to find a sense of peace and balance in a world that held none for me. I didn't live day to day. I existed moment to moment. I lived in New York City then and was aware of a holistic center called the Open Center. That's where I took many of my workshops.

The first one I took was in Shamanism. When I became aware of Reiki, I was attuned to Level 1, and later, I attended the workshops that I mentioned before. I read books about crystals and candle magic. I looked to any modality that could help me claw my way to a point where I could begin to heal myself. Until that happened, my work focused on personal healing. Eventually, heal I did, and in doing so, I learned for myself what worked for me and what didn't.

One of the modalities I read about and used at home (NOTE: THIS IS NOT A REIKI ADD-ON) was candle magic. Did you know that every time you sit before a birthday cake and blow out the candles, you are doing part of a ceremony used in candle magic? Of course, 99% of what the practitioner does you skip. To use another cliché, you cut to the chase. You made a wish and blew out the candle.

Again, I simplify and what I say may make a true practitioner of candle magic cringe. I don't know if what I did was right or wrong according to a real practitioner.

I read part of a book.

I did what I did.

It helped.

Without any real knowledge or understanding of candle magic, but knowing my need for personal healing was great, I charged the candle with my intention. I stood before it and meditated to Universe. I asked her to help me find the peace and balance I was searching for. I placed a little oil in my palms and rubbed them over the candle. I charged the candle with that intent and asked it to send those intentions out to Universe. Then I lit the candle. Ideally, you let the candle burn down. But I was using a 7-day candle and had two cats. I snuffed out the candle (I read you never should blow it out) at night and the following evening, I charged it again (minus the oil because it was now in a glass container) and lit it.

I began to believe in, and accept as my truth, that there are many things in this world that must be accepted on faith. When I completed my personal candle ceremony and sat on my bed watching the flame, I breathed easier. I knew that even though I had no real idea what I was doing, what I did felt right and proper for me to do at that point in my life. When I felt that I didn't have to know how something worked, but knew in my heart that work it did, that was when my healing began to take hold.

The flame on that candle helped send my thoughts, my intentions, out to Universe, to reach Spirit, to reach Reiki. An idea birthed itself within me. Universe does not need a structure for a person to have an individual relationship with it. I don't remember the actual turning point, but before that first candle burned down completely, I noticed that I stopped walking around my apartment listening to the hammering sounds of the silent rooms and whispering to myself, "forever."

Now, back to Aromatherapy. People all over the world practice and use essential oils, and these people are on the same path as I. I knew with the same assurance that I know Reiki is Reiki, the oils worked in harmony with Universe, and for our higher good. I had no idea how they worked; I just accepted that they did. I trusted.

Knowing what I just said to be part of my truth, how could I not add an additional factor, lavender oil, to my healing environment? Even if after I lit the candle under the bowl and forgot about it, remembering only to add a little more water sometimes, how could I not use it. It could only help. It couldn't hurt. It didn't matter if I had no idea what lavender oil did or how it did it. It didn't matter if lavender oil did not empower me because I was not an aromatherapist. I didn't endeavor to make aromatherapy in integral part of my sessions like I did with scanning. But I also felt it would be foolish to ignore an accepted modality when that modality could add to the general welfare of my students or clients. What did empower me was knowing that I was doing everything I could to enhance my session or workshop. If I had the knowledge to use the oils, I would have. If you have the knowledge, I offer for your consideration the following meditation, though I doubt if you need it. You're probably using the oils anyway.

Go to the Reiki Energy and ask how I can add my knowledge of essential oils into my Reiki practice. (Please, if you know of any other healing modality and are curious if that could be adapted to work with Reiki, change the question and go to Reiki.)

Or

Meditate to the oil (I'd select your favorite) and ask the same question. How can I use my knowledge in you, in essential oils, to enhance my Reiki practice?

Add-On
Tapping the Thymus

Ladles and Jellyspoons
I come before you, to stand behind you,
To tell you something I know nothing about.
Next Thursday, which is Good Friday,
There will be a mothers' meeting for fathers' only.
Admission is free, pay at the door,
Pull up a seat and sit on the floor.
We will be discussing the four corners of the round table.
Author: Anonymous

What does this unknown author's poem mean to me? Absolutely nothing. I have read several other versions and all of them state the same nothing as this. Why did I use it? I thought it would be a wonderful introduction to tapping the thymus, something I readily admit, like Anonymous, I know nothing about.

The little I know is that the thymus is an organ in the upper chest cavity. It has to do with the immune system, works with white blood cells and is part of the lymphatic system.

I learned that the thymus existed many years ago when a student who I was attuning to Level 2 (she had her Level 1 training elsewhere) asked a simple question. "Why do I have to tap my thymus before I start every session. I don't like doing it."

My answer was simple, seeing as I had no idea what the

thymus was. "I don't know," I said. Then I asked her why she did it.

Her answer was also simple. "I was told I had to do it before I begin a Reiki session."

We then discussed it. She told me a little about the thymus organ and that her Reiki I teacher said that when a person taps the thymus, it stimulates the white blood cells. They are the healing cells - they defend the body against diseases. Accepting the validity of the statement that tapping does stimulate the cells, I could understand why her former teacher included it in the level 1 workshop. It would strengthen the practitioner. But as I write this, I realize that my student never said whether or not her teacher asked her to tell the clients to do the same. It would make sense if the teacher did.

For me, this would be a minor matter. If it doesn't feel right, don't do it. But it also begs the answer to an important question, which is why I am including this section in the book. Why did she do it even if it didn't feel right to her? And that answer is not simple.

Stepping away from Reiki for a moment, I bring the following up for your consideration. Most of us have spent our early lives in school and we were all taught that what the teacher teaches is what we have to learn. Also, no matter what our job in life is, there are times when we are called on to act as teachers, explaining to someone how to do a task we perform. Many times the how we do a task is a set series of steps. If you wish to change the oil in your car, you do it the way you were taught. The nature or structure of this task is dictated by what has to be done for the task to be accomplished correctly.

In our society, we tend to accept what a "teacher" says as an absolute. The thirty-two years I spent before retiring were spent as a teacher in a middle school, sixth and seventh grades, ages ranging between eleven and thirteen. I taught history and English. There is little or no creativity in history. It happened already. There is a lot of creativity in English, especially in writing. But there is hardly any creativity when it comes to basics: capitals, periods, grammar, etc. I taught it. My students had to learn it as I taught it.

The "teacher" is a person who knows more about the subject than you or I do. The "teacher" knows the best way something has to be learned. Therefore, we think, I need to understand and do what the "teacher" tells us.

Many times, like changing the oil or writing a complete sentence, copying the teacher holds true. But many times it doesn't and shouldn't. It has been said that in polite conversations, you should never discuss three topics: sex, politics and religion. If you have ever had discussions on any of these, you know that they can quickly turn into arguments. The reason is that all three of these topics immediately elicit an emotional response. That response may override any logic you may wish to use to state an opinion different from the person you are speaking to.

Whether a professional teacher or just being asked to show a person how to do something, we should be able to know if the way we are teaching is because that is the way it must be done (like changing the oil) or is it the way we want it to be done? And what happens when we are asked to show a person something where individual creativity is a factor? Should an art teacher say, "This is the way you must paint the human body," or should the teacher say, "This is the way I paint the human body."

I believe whoever is in the role of a teacher should accept the responsibility to make sure they separate from within themselves the "you must do it this way" from the "I want you to do it this way." They owe that to the person they are teaching. The problem is that the distinction is so blurred that the "you must" overrides the "I want," especially when the teacher is emotionally attached to the outcome.

How does this apply to Reiki and the thymus? The Level 1

certificates I gave to my students reads as follows:

Reiki
USUI SHIKI RYOHO
This is to certify that
(Name)
has completed the
First Degree in the
Usui System of Natural Healing

Dr. Usui's name appears on the certificate. I haven't seen any other practitioners' certificates, but I assume that Dr. Usui's name is also on theirs. When people read about Reiki for the first time, they learn about Dr. Usui, who he was and the fact that he brought modern day Reiki into our world. It is impossible to hold a Level 1 workshop regardless if the RMT (Reiki Master Teacher) is a traditional RMT or a nontraditional teacher) without hearing about the father of Reiki, Dr. Usui.

I am making the case that Reiki can be generic or personal. I believe that most people expect to be taught generic Reiki because that is what Dr. Usui gave us.

My question is, should a Reiki Master include thymus tapping in the list of "musts" that a practitioner should do without mentioning it's an add-on and leaving that up to the student? You know my answer. No.

Should a Reiki Master include that tapping in a list of things their students could do (after hearing from them the why they should) if they felt that is was "right" for them? Definitely.

I mentioned earlier that when I spoke to my students about some of the add-ons I use, I explained that they are not part of traditional Reiki. After telling my students why I used them, I left the decision to use or not to use up to them. I believe that all Reiki Master Teachers should accept the same responsibility of informing their students what is and what is not Usui's Reiki.

If you have attended any level workshop of Reiki and you were told that you must perform a certain act before, during or immediately after you do Reiki, and what you were told doesn't sit well with you, then don't do it. If just stopping makes you feel uncomfortable, I suggest you meditate to Reiki and find out from the source what is best.

Will not tapping the thymus change the nature of Reiki? No.

Will tapping the thymus change the way you look at Reiki if you don't wish to? Yes.

Remember, the basic philosophy in Reiki has not changed since Dr. Usui came down from the mountain. Reiki does what Reiki does. You cannot do Reiki incorrectly. Add-ons cannot change the nature of Reiki. I think they add to her, but you must make up your own mind.

Also, you must be aware of this because I believe it is very important and another main reason for including this section. I said earlier, "In our society, we tend to accept what a "teacher" says as an absolute." Reiki is not an absolute. Even traditional RMTs agree that in certain areas, individual differences are acceptable. It is YOUR responsibility to decide if what your RMT says is in the "you must" or the "I want" category. If you are not sure ask, "Why do I have to do this?" In life, a question not asked is an answer not given. You would not pass a steak knife to another person blade facing out or blade in your hand, sharp side facing into your palm even if someone told you to do it that way. Do not let someone tell you how to hold Reiki, whether they are traditionalist or nontraditionalist. In Reiki, teachers, including me, are not absolute!

There are no meditation connected to this section unless you decide you wish to do one. I believe that when you followed the meditations in the Structure Vs. Intuition section, and you asked what was most and least important, you would have discovered anything that did not empower you. If you wish, you can repeat that meditation. Additionally, if you are a doctor or nurse or any person who knows anatomy or has any medical training, and taping the thymus strikes a chord with you, by all means, add it to you basket of knowledge.

Add-On
Shamanic Reiki

This is a major add-on, one of the most powerful and empowering for me. So much so that I could fill a book with it. As a matter of fact, I did. Along with my co-author, Llyn Roberts, we created the book, "Shamanic Reiki: Expanded Ways of Working with Universal Life Force Energy". The purpose of that book is to explain in detail how to incorporate shamanic techniques into your Reiki Sessions. The difference between the two books is in this text, the thrust is to empower you, the practitioner. In Shamanic Reiki, the thrust is to empower not only the practitioner but also the client. Both Llyn and I believe that empowering both is a significant factor in promoting personal healing.

There is too much involved in incorporating shamanic techniques in a Reiki session to include it in this text. But if the idea of integrating the two modalities, Reiki and Shamanism resonates within you, I suggest you read our book.

Why Practitioners May Become Disenchanted with Reiki

Have you ever felt that Reiki wasn't working properly or that you weren't channeling Reiki correctly? Though I have discussed this before, the following section covers what has been missed so far. If you are a practitioner who finds your enthusiasm waning or if you still are committed to Reiki but need to find ways of deepening your commitment, the solution to both are the same, empowering yourself. In September of 2012, several people within a short time of each other contacted me and asked for my help in reconnecting to Reiki. And one of them was a Reiki

Master. Thus did Spirit's whisper prod me into writing this book?

You have read many ways that can help you achieve personal empowerment since you began reading. What I would like to do now is address a specific reason why you may either feel disconnected to Reiki or why you the need to strengthen a connection that you have now. There must be something gnawing at you, Spirit's whispering to you, as I have called it, letting you know that something is not right.

While writing this book, I received an email from a gentleman I was working with, Steve from California. He was a disenchanted practitioner. Steve wrote:

> "I think my disappointment with Reiki was mostly due to the lack of a measurable, observable response. I read in the Reiki books about people feeling energy move or seeing energy flowing. The implications are that when you receive Reiki, you will feel it, experience it. Suddenly you will see auras, feel energy flowing and see people being healed. When that doesn't happen I feel disconnected. I wonder, maybe Reiki didn't work."

Curing Vs. Healing

Steve's problem is a common one and I am sure that beginning Level 1 practitioners feel that all the time. The part of his email I want to deal with first is his thought that without an observable response, it is easy to accept the idea that Reiki doesn't work. That statement is part of a much broader topic that I always included in my workshops. The discussions center around what is the difference between curing and healing. It is of the utmost importance in your understanding of Reiki that you realize that difference and know the answers to: Does Reiki cure? Does Reiki heal?

Are the two the same?

No.

In our world there are many religions. Suppose that in one religion, all prayers would be answered within twenty-four hours. Pray for a new job on Monday and by Tuesday, you found it. Need a new car? Pray after yours broke down and within a day, you're driving again. If that were so, do you think most people would convert?

If a belief (especially in any Spiritual context) in "something" worked all the time with all the people who believed it, I think that everyone would know what that "something" is and would practice it. But no belief works all the time with all the people. Opinion. So say I.

What is the difference between curing and healing? Being cured means you are free from the condition. I mentioned Mrs. Takata earlier in the text. According to Wikipedia, she suffered from several illnesses, including gallstones, an abdominal tumor and appendicitis. After several months of Reiki treatments, those conditions disappeared. She was cured.

Healing, on the other hand, does not have to mean being cured. Mrs. Takata was cured and of course, healed. If you are cured, you are healed. But the opposite is not true. If you are healed, you may not be cured. So what does healing mean if a person is not cured?

You are healed if you are one with "What is". (If you are accepting the present situation.)

You are healed if you are living in the present.

You are healed if you are in harmony with the condition, even if that condition is fatal. The patient with incurable cancer will probably not be cured by Reiki. But with help from the Reiki practitioner, that person can be healed. That person, when receptive to the love, understanding, and compassion of Reiki Energy, can come to accept the outcome without fear. Not easy, but possible.

The example I always used in my classes was the story of Christopher Reeve. In May 1995, Christopher fell off a horse. The accident resulted in paralysis that lasted for the remainder of his life. For Christopher to be cured one thing had to happen - he had to be able to walk. He never did.

But I contend that he was healed. He became one with his illness. He accepted the "What is" and continued his life from that point of view. He could have hated his life, his God, his doctors and the people around him. He could have turned into a recluse, hermiting himself in his home, feeling so sorry for himself that his only wish was to die. He may have, and probably did have some or all of those feelings at one time or another. But he moved passed them. I have no idea of the process he used in his healing, but there came a day when he decided to live in the present. Working with his wife, he founded The Christopher Reeve Foundation and co-founded The Reeve-Irvine Research Center. He made time to lobby on behalf of everyone who suffered from spinal cord injuries. He lobbied congress to approve embryonic stem cell research. He and his wife traveled, gave interviews and he hosted the Paralympics in Atlanta, Georgia. For his efforts, in August of 1996, Time Magazine placed his picture on their cover. Christopher Reeve lived the rest of his life to its fullest. For me, that meant he was healed.

You're asking, "What does this have to do with nothing happening during Reiki?"

To be empowered by Reiki you have to accept the outcome of the Reiki Energy.

You should not feel badly if you do not feel any energy moving through your hands. Many beginning Reiki practitioners do not. But as their relationship with Reiki grows, their confidence and trust in her builds, they will. There were many days, many sessions when I did not feel anything, even after I became a Reiki Master. Feeling the energy is not a guarantee.

You should not feel badly if after the session when you ask the client how he/she feels, the answer is just, "I guess OK."

You should not feel badly if after working with a client for a month, the condition has not improved. You may have to switch your efforts by discussing with your client the prospects of being healed, not cured.

When clients or students in any level workshop asked me, "Does Reiki cure?

My answer, "Sometimes."

When they asked, "Does Reiki heal?"

My answer, "Sometimes. Just like feeling the energy, the outcome of Reiki is never guaranteed."

When they asked, "Why didn't anything happen?"

My answer, "Something always happens."

When you pray to Deity for something, and you get no answer, is it possible that no answer is the answer? Yes.

Universal Life Force Energy enters a person and does what is in the best interest or higher good of that person. If Reiki Energy does not cure or even allow healing, could that be in the best interest or higher good of that person? Yes.

Could it be that sometimes, for whatever reason, you do not feel any energy leaving your hands? Yes.

Could it be that your client feels nothing. Yes.

Could it be our fault as practitioners that no major movement occurred within the client? No.

Will we ever know the reason we think nothing happened? No.

Did "nothing happen." No.

If something happened, what?

Whatever Reiki wanted to happen because that is the nature of Reiki. Reiki does all the work, remember?

I have also said that Reiki will shape itself around your definition and you even meditated on that. But Reiki will not compromise herself by discarding her role in the curing/healing process. What Reiki does, Reiki does. Reiki will allow us to change how we use her because in changing that, we empower ourselves. But we cannot change the effect Reiki has. We cannot alter Reiki's decision regarding the outcome. That is her domain, always has been, always will be. But I know that her decision, even if it is in the negative, will be done within the scope of her love, understanding, and compassion for all of us.

When people conceive that nothing is happening, they don't think that what IS happening is what Reiki dictates must happen. Nothing, according to me, is something. I just don't know what that something is. Do you stop believing in Deity when you pray for something and don't get it?

A negative outcome does make things much harder for the practitioner as well as the client. We need to council the client in order to accept the "what is" of the situation. And that is not easy. It takes time, experience, and lots of patience.

Part of your process in empowering yourself is coming to terms with what I have just said. You must decide if what you just read resonates with you. If not, you have to come up with your own way of accepting the outcome of a session or series of sessions. I don't know how you can be completely empowered by Reiki if you cannot state that you are in harmony with any end result.

You are not happy when you don't feeling any energy coming from your hands. Or when a first time client says nothing happened and never returns, or when you don't like the outcome of any Reiki session. But you must accept it. Reiki allows you to be you when you perform Reiki. You must allow Reiki to be Reiki.

If you believe that you were deficient in some way and caused the negative outcome, how can you become One with Reiki? I have said it before and I say it again now. Reiki does all the work. If you truly believe that Reiki will do no harm, that belief must include the times when we cannot perceive the "no harm" because the condition does not seem to improve or gets worse or when that client said nothing happened and never came back.

What I suggest is a single meditation. Go to either Reiki

Energy or your symbol. From within, ask the following:

What advice can you give me regarding the meaning of
Curing and Healing?

If what you discover during this meditation is not in complete
harmony with you, ask from within the meditation:

How may I incorporate what I have learned into my definition of Reiki?

Again, if you are not satisfied after discussing this with Reiki,
Ask:

What must I do to accept a negative outcome? (I am sorry for
presuming to answer for Reiki, but don't be surprised if the
answer is, "Pay the price.")

In the section on scanning, I said, "I need to know that I am more
than nothing" when I do Reiki. And so do you. It's my belief that
those negative feelings we have about ourselves come from our
egos. They, the egos, don't like knowing that they aren't doing
anything. They want to see a positive result after a Reiki session
so they can say what wonderful healers they/we are. It is the ego
that plants the idea into us that Reiki is not working. You can
overcome that by being fully empowered by Reiki. The following
is another way.

I am going to suggest an additional mediation if you feel it
will help you. I'd like to inform that the origin of this
meditation is NOT within Reiki. It has its roots in the shamanic
belief that we can meditate to and get information from different
aspects of ourselves. If you decide it is something you would like
to try, please do so. If not, don't. I suggest you meditate to your
ego.

Begin as you always have by going to Reiki Energy. I remind you to breathe in the energy as you did in the very beginning so you will feel safe, secure and completely surrounded by the love, understanding, and compassion of Reiki. When you are ready, ask the Reiki Energy to bring forth into her light, your ego, in a shape of a human being. Within the safety of the Reiki Energy, ask your ego the following.

Why can't you accept that we cannot affect the outcome of any Reiki session?
How can we compromise so I will not feel badly when I don't think anything is happening and you create that feeling when we don't know what is happening?
What do I have to give up or do to make this compromise?
What will you give up to make this compromise?

I don't want you to break this meditation into two. You need to dialog with your ego and find out what has to happen for the ego to remain the ego while allowing Reiki to be Reiki. At the end of this meditation, thank your ego for coming and sharing with you.

Expectations

Many years ago, I saw a news story about why calling or writing a politician can be very effective. My thought was why would any politician consider one person's opinion. The answer was really eye opening. The story said that they completed a study that showed for every one letter or phone call a politician receives, 9 other people feel the same but either they are too lazy to write or have an idea exactly equal to mine. That meant if a politician received 1000 letters and calls supporting (or not) an issue, 10,000 of his constituents agreed. You read in Steve's mail something I haven't written about because to be honest, I never thought about it. It deals with expectations people might have before becoming attuned to Reiki. Yet, I don't believe that his concern is unique - it just never occurred to me until now.

Steve questioned the difference between his expectations (feeling or seeing energy and auras) and that when doing Reiki, those expectations were not met. When they weren't, the seed of disconnection could have been planted and the idea that Reiki wasn't working could have been born. He, as did I (and I am certain that many of you) read of other peoples' experiences how Reiki effected them. To that short list, I will also add that some people say that after their attunement, they become more psychic.

Though I have dealt with some of his concerns throughout the text, (like feeling energy) I thought it wise to specifically address the topic of expectations. The issue is what should a person realistically expect to feel/see/experience regarding Reiki when they receive their attunements and how those expectation can effect your relationship with Reiki. The answer is relatively simple but as with everything else in this text, you can't just take my word for it.

What expectations should you have when you become a Reiki practitioner?

None!

By now you know that in seeking a Reiki that is personalized by her to you, your experience in Reiki may be unique. The progressive order that others say happened to them may not happen to you. Both ways are correct. Yours for your Reiki and theirs for their Reiki.

Do I think people experienced feeling, seeing energy and auras? Yes.

Do I think they happen to everyone? No

Did they happen to me? Feeling energy, yes, though I don't remember if I felt it from the very beginning. Seeing energy, auras or have a heightened psychic sense, no.

Did it matter that I didn't experience those things. No.

Why? First, I never had any expectations when I began Reiki.

Second, and here is where I repeat myself again, my relationship to Reiki is personal. It doesn't matter how others react to her. It only matter how I react to her. All that matters is how YOU react to her. Pay the price!

In my personal life, I try not to have expectations because if I expect something then instead of being fully present to "what is", I am present to what I want the "what is" to be. A philosophy I try to adhere to. I am amenable to most things in life as long as they don't involve eating creamed spinach. But, as my goddaughter will attest to, when we went to a New York restaurant noted for its fine cooking and she wasn't feeling well, all she ordered was creamed spinach. To her surprise, I tasted a small amount of it. Even though I knew I would probably not like the dish because I have never tasted any version of it that I did, I am open to the possibility that there might be a recipe I do like. If I refused to try it, then I would be living in the past, allowing my past experiences to govern how I will react to a similar situations in the present. The small taste did not harm me - it just reinforced the validity of my philosophy. But without tasting it, I would not have known that. Of course, I am in no way advocating you adopt my philosophy. What works for me . . . remember? World wide, there are probably 100s of millions of people who like creamed spinach. The fact I'm not one of them should not bother them when they enjoy it - and their enjoying it does not bother me.

You have read so much and done so much by the time you reach this point in the book that you know I want you to discover what works for you, what is in harmony with you. What occurs with other people is something you can look forward to. But don't have the expectation that because they experience something, you will too. By opening yourself up to the possibilities Reiki can hold for you, by looking for your personal answers and not accepting the answers of others, you empower yourself. I have never seen an aura and it has never bothered me. Why?

I have seen Reiki and so have you.

I have communicated with her and received my answers from her.

And so have you.

That's all I need.

That is all we need.

If you have expectations, try to release them and be present to what Reiki is telling you. This may not be easy, but look to the affirmatives you have received from Reiki for strength in releasing what has not been affirmed. And if you are just starting your Reiki and nothing seems to be happening, if it is hard to trust yourself, then trust me. You will feel the energy. You will feel the power of Reiki. You just have to begin building your relationship with her. As with all relationships, they take time to mature.

When you merged with Reiki Energy in the first meditation, you felt her power. You felt her energy. I asked you to remember that feeling and bring it with you to your Reiki sessions. I said that when a Reiki practitioner is ready to channel the energy, all that is needed is a thought to Universe, to Reiki, that you now wish the energy to begin to flow. Many times I feel the energy in my hands, many times, I don't. When I do Reiki, for most of the session, I repeat the following mantra to myself. "Reiki Reiki Reiki. Cho Ku Rei Cho Ku Rei Cho Ku Rei, over and over, over and over. This does two things for me. It helps me focus - keeps my mind from wandering. But more important, it reminds me and helps me recall the feeling I had the first time I merged with Reiki. How you tell Universe you are ready to channel Reiki is up to you. But if you recall the feeling you had when you entered Reiki's energy for the first time and you bring that energy back into our reality, I truly believe that you will feel the heat of her energy in your hands and know that you are truly connected to Reiki.

If you wish, I give you a simple meditation. Select an expectation you had/have that has not been meet. Meditate to either your symbol or Reiki Energy and ask:

Why can't I reach my expectation and . . . (state the expectation)? What holds me back?
What has to happen for me to reach my expectation?
Repeat this either within this mediation or in a separate one with each expectation (or disappointment) you have regarding Reiki and performing it.

Waiting Time Between Attunements

This section raises what I have always thought of as a non-issue. But not knowing what you consider issues or not, I am including it. It does not deal with empowerment or your personal relationship with Reiki. It deals only with a structure that may be placed on you and for most people that structure may be minor. If you ever find yourself in the position where the structure is confining, then there is an option I suggest for your consideration. The only validity to what I write now will be my personal experience.

The following is the general procedure that traditional RMTs use in allowing their students to progress from one level to the next. After a student receives the Level 1 attunement, the RMT may wait a minimum of ninety days to schedule a Level 2 workshop with those students. After Level 2, the waiting period for Level 3 can be up to a year or longer.

However, my life dictated that I could not accept the traditional waiting time. When I became a Level 2 practitioner I knew I could not wait the required time after receiving my Level 1. At that time, I had no idea that there were major controversies between traditional and nontraditional Reiki. I was only aware of doing what was best for me.

A traditional Reiki Master attuned me to Level 1 in February

1996. During this time, my liver enzymes were elevated. My doctor felt that the elevated levels were due to switching cholesterol medication without waiting for the old medicine to be completely gone from my system. But the level remained high and after four or five months, he wanted me to have a liver biopsy, just to make sure nothing serious was occurring. The biopsy was scheduled for April 10 or 11. I wanted my Level 2 before then.

Do you remember what I told you about accepting the word of the "teacher?" Was I no different from anyone else? At my Level 1 workshop, my Reiki teacher told us we had to wait ninety days if we wished a Level 2 attunement.

I would have to wait.

But I could not wait. I didn't have ninety days.

In searching for other alternatives, I looked in several of the free magazines usually available in health food stores and holistic centers. I read the advertisements Reiki Masters placed regarding their workshops. That's the first time I found out that not all Reiki was done in the same way. I saw ads where Reiki Masters offered two days workshops covering both Reiki I and II. I even saw one or two Reiki Masters giving a three-day workshop covering all Reiki Levels. I do admit I was very confused and had many of questions that I could not answer.

Since being attuned, I had performed Reiki on myself. It relaxed me and made me feel a little better. (This was slightly more than a year after my wife died and I was still in miserable shape.) I did it on my cats. One could lie on me for almost half an hour before getting off my chest. The other didn't care for Reiki and usually got up after only a few minutes. I did Reiki for a few of my friends. I didn't consider the proper hand positions, I just did Reiki. I was in my infancy regarding Reiki and hadn't even begun to decide how I would eventually perform it.

If my teacher wouldn't attune me to Level 2 (though in his defense, I never asked. I just assumed he would say no), I had to find another teacher. After a few calls to the Reiki Masters who advertised, I did. His name was Stephen Scheld. Though he did not have any workshops scheduled, he agreed to come to my house and attune me. He also said that he had another student who wanted her Level 3, and if I wanted it in the future, he would attune both of us at the same time. When he came, I asked him the questions that gnawed at me about Reiki in general and specifically the time issue that existed. He, being a nontraditional Reiki Master, answered them in his truth and his truth resonated within me. Universe works in her own time and her own way, and on April 8, 1996, I was attuned to Level 2. (I was attuned to the Master Level along with Stephen's other student on July 21st.)

Either on the 10th or 11th of April, I went to the hospital in the morning and had my liver biopsy. After it was over, I had to remain lying on the bed for five or six hours. It was explained to me that they had to make sure the liver was not bleeding. They attached an automatic blood pressure machine to my arm and every fifteen minutes it beeped and took my blood pressure. I remember the first time the nurse came and read the pressure. Then she asked me if I wanted some pain medication.

I said, I think, "What for?"

She said, "For the pain."

I said, "What pain?"

This little conversation went on two or three more times. Then she just came and wrote the pressure numbers on my chart.

To be honest, I don't remember doing Reiki on myself. I received the attunement to use Level 2 Reiki on the pain I was sure I was going to have and since I didn't have any pain, I didn't think of using Reiki. Did the attunement I had two or three days before protect me or keep the pain from coming? I don't know. I do know a friend of mine with major liver problems had five or six liver biopsies and always had varying degrees of pain or discomfort, I had neither. But, if you ask me did I believe the Reiki attunement was a major factor in how I felt, my answer is yes.

Though I would not have been able to say the following at that point in time, I can say it now. The experience began to build my personal relationship with Reiki. Remember, I was only attuned to Level 1 about two months prior to the biopsy. I knew that my attunement was not in keeping with the general flow of attunements. Yet it didn't matter. I believed that the ease of my procedure was due to the attunement. Looking back with hindsight, this was the first time I asked Reiki to do something that was not in keeping with what I was told was a "must do." Without realizing it, I asked Reiki to overlook the time discrepancy and allow the Level 2 attunement to help me deal with the after effects of the biopsy.

Reiki listened.

Why did I bring it up? Some of you might need help in deciding the timing of your attunements and should be aware that the issue of structure or not permeates all aspects of Reiki, even dictating when you can be attuned to Levels 2 and 3.

If you are unaware that other options exist, then you will accept, as I did, the teacher is the teacher.

If that is not within your comfort zone, if like me, you have a need or just want to continue sooner than the traditional time frame allows, you can, if you wish, find a teacher who will be compatible with your desire.

If the above issue is a concern for you, I suggest you meditate and asked either Reiki Energy or your symbol about following the time line your traditional RMT puts forth or seeking an alternative.

The Extra Attunement

I told you once that the main purpose of a Level 3 workshop is to instruct you how to attune others into Reiki. This means that as a general rule, you have a desire to become a RMT. But becoming a RMT is NOT a requirement. There are many Reiki Masters who have decided, some even before they were attuned, that they do not wish to become teachers of Reiki. For them, becoming a Master is part of their personal journey. When I became a Reiki Master, I had no intention of becoming a teacher. That idea came much later. I was attuned to Level 3 because I wanted to continue my self-healing process.

I believe the idea a person must have a desire to teach began with Mrs. Takata. She asked those twenty-two people she attuned to the Master level to promise that they would, from that point on, derive their income solely from teaching Reiki. A heavy burden, but one the twenty-two agreed to.

Being a Master intensifies Reiki Energy and of course, increases a person's knowledge of Reiki. Becoming a Master is in itself a powerful act of empowerment. But if you don't wish to be a RMT, or if you planned to and that plan never realized itself, please know, there is absolutely no reason why you should not take your Master workshop or that you should feel that you are any less of a Reiki Master because you are not a RMT.

Aside from healing, Reiki is a philosophy, a way of looking at life, and being a Reiki Master adds strength and direction to that philosophy. I have not included anything about living in the light of Reiki in this book because that is not the book's purpose.

Throughout this text, I have always I offered you information and asked you to decide what is best for you. I have never said, Listen to me, do the following my way. I break with that now. "Listen to me, do the following my way!"

Many traditional Reiki Masters adhere to Mrs. Takata's original fee schedule: $150 for Reiki I, $500 for Reiki II, and $10,000 for Reiki III. In dealing with economic reality, many of those Reiki Masters added an additional fourth workshop to the entire attunement process. This is a Reiki Master workshop but does not include any information on how to attune others. It will attune you to Dai Ko Myo, the Reiki Master symbol, include information about the symbol and other things the Reiki Master will add, but by the end of the workshop, you will not have the knowledge that other Reiki Masters have. For this non-teaching Master workshop, the charge can be as high as $2,000 to $3,000. Please, DO NOT DO THIS. I am not sure what Reiki Masters' call this type of workshop. But all should explain before you sign up that they will not teach you how to attune others to Reiki.

My annoyance with this is on several levels. First, this type of attunement will disenfranchise you. Being an almost Reiki Master may make you feel that the Reiki you do is not equal to the Reiki other Masters do. That attitude will denigrate your sense of empowerment, the power of your own Reiki and your feelings of self worth regarding Reiki. This will tear down what I have spent this entire book building up. A friend who was attuned in this type of workshop, when she found out I was a Reiki Master, said something like, "I am too, except I can't attune other people." Why the exception? She felt she wasn't on the same level as I was. In performing Reiki, she WAS just same as I, as all Reiki Masters are. But when she said, "Except I can't attune other people," she was downgrading herself.

Second, for less than the amount you may be charged for this type of workshop, you can find a Reiki Master who will attune you to Level 3 and you will be given all the information all Reiki Masters are supposed to have.

If you cannot afford what your Reiki Master wishes to charge for the full workshop, find another teacher. I think my Reiki Master charged $400 for my Level 3. I usually charged $335. A good resource for finding a Master Level Workshop is the one I gave you before; William Rand's "The International Center for Reiki Training" (http://www.reiki.org.) I know he gives workshops in various US cities and may even hold them or be able to guide you if you live outside the US. I think his total cost is approximately $850. Even though I have never met William, I have read some of his work and I trust his integrity. A second place would be the free newspapers or magazines that are usually found in health food stores and/or holistic centers. That's how I found my Reiki Master, remember?

And finally, and this is what eats at my stomach lining the most. This kind of workshop is given by traditional Reiki Masters who know their economic opportunities are very limited holding fast to Mrs. Takata's fee schedule. But instead of lowering their price for the Master Level workshop to make it reachable to the vast majority of people, they alter the workshop! Highly nontraditional. To my knowledge, being made a partial Reiki Master was not available to the twenty-two Reiki Masters Mrs. Takata attuned. This says to me that the Reiki Masters who offer this type of workshop feel it is perfectly acceptable to insist that pure Reiki is attained only by following Mrs. Takata's teachings. But when it really affects them, on a personal and economical level, it is perfectly acceptable to make an exception to this rule. A big exception. A very big exception!

I repeat, please do not pay for a workshop that will not give you everything you need. It will not empower you - it may even help in disconnecting you with Reiki because you may begin to think you are an inferior Master because you did not receive a full workshop and cannot attune people. This also applies to those of you I mentioned in the beginning of this section, who know you don't wish to become RMTs. Having the knowledge of being a Reiki Master without the "except" will remove from you any thought of also being a lesser Master because you don't teach.

I often speak about Spirit's whisper, never about Spirit's shout. Universal Life Force Energy, Reiki, Spirit, Deity, our Divine Soul believe in free will, free choice. In the matter of being attuned to Level 3, choose wisely.

Attunements - Self Doubts

I said I became a Reiki Master in July of 1996. After that, I continued doing Reiki for my friends and of course my cats. But I didn't really consider teaching Reiki for almost five more years.

When I knew I was ready to teach, I had to plan what I would do in my workshop. I had "Reiki: The Healing Touch First & Second Degree Manual" by William Rand. Since that was the workbook I received for my Level 2 and I liked it, I knew I would use that for both levels. Also, I had William's Master Level workbook plus the notes I made during my Level 3 attunement.

By this time, the Internet was out of its infancy, Dot com companies were constantly popping up, and I was getting used to my new Macintosh computer. Because of my teaching experience, I wanted to research the attunement process so I could have as much information as I could get before I decided how I would teach my workshops.

When I began my Reiki career, the inner workings of Reiki were supposed to be a secret. Rarely did I see on-line or in Reiki books the names of the symbols. Writers just referred to them by their function, the power symbol, the mental health symbol, and the distant healing symbol. It was as if Reiki were an exclusive club and all that was missing was a secret handshake. One of the first books (to my knowledge) that cracked that barrier was "Essential Reiki: A Complete Guide to an Ancient Healing Art" by Diane Stein. She not only named names, but diagramed the symbols too.

By the early 2000s and by searching the web, I found several Reiki Masters who had placed the Reiki manuals they used (and for the most part, wrote) for their classes on-line for all to read. They demystified the attunement process. Earlier I asked some of you to Google Reiki and Karuna Reiki symbols.

I didn't give you a website.

In the beginning there weren't any. Now there are many.

Reiki is fluid. Reiki is changing. Google can supply you with all the websites you need.

I held my first workshop in January 2001. It went fine. But

even with the nontraditional attitude I had adopted, I was concerned that my attunements might not take. Maybe I didn't remember the symbols correctly; maybe I didn't put them in the proper places and use the proper order. What if I forgot a step and didn't realize it? I worried about the attunements even as I was giving them.

But I shouldn't have. In speaking to the participants after the workshop and in having follow-up conversations with them, everything worked just the way it should.

Again, you might be asking yourself what's the purpose of this section. I wanted to share this with you. Even though I had firm beliefs regarding the power of personal intention, I still doubted. I still wondered, what if... Even though I had an open mind, a nagging thought hung on my mind's hook. The teacher is the teacher and what if I didn't do it right. It took several workshops for me to loose that thought and replace it with I WAS the teacher and what I did was exactly what I was supposed to do. Your knowing that I was doubting, your knowing that even I was finding it hard to "Pay the price" when I first stepped into the role of Reiki Master Teacher, may make it easier for you to struggle through paying your own price. And if you are, like I was, a fledging RMT who is holding your first workshop, after the workshop is over, allow those doubts to enter your conscious mind. As you recall each doubt, remember the feeling you had when you entered Reiki Energy for the first time. Then ask yourself, "Would that Reiki allow my attunement to be incorrect?" I wish I had done that after my first workshop.

If you still have any doubts with any aspect of Reiki, please know that they are normal. In time, you will work through them all and whatever Reiki you are left with is the Reiki you are left with. Your Reiki.

The Purpose of Reiki

For me, Reiki is in a constant state of evolvement, moving from where it is today to where it will be tomorrow and the countless tomorrows after it. I do not believe it can or should remain static.

I do not say that if you are practicing Reiki or if you are a Reiki Master Teacher and have had many wonderful and powerful workshops, you should change anything you do because of what you have read in this book.

I do say that no matter what you level of Reiki you are on, no matter how you relate to Reiki, you should always be able to listen to suggestions that might help you further your own Reiki. If no areas exist - then no areas exist. If the Reiki you do is the Reiki you need to do, then all is well. But if something I said causes the slightest itch inside you and you mutter the sound, "Hmm," then maybe you might like to add that something to your basket of knowledge. Knowledge never hurts and if you ever find yourself in a position where you don't feel right about anything you do in Reiki, maybe you can use your knowledge and do something about it.

I now pose a question to you and I have waited until almost the end of this text because I believe you should have a solid relationship with Reiki before meditating on this. You meditated once on the definition of Reiki. You asked her what are your limits? What are your boundaries? I don't know if your answers and mine were the same. If not, we were both correct. The meditation I wish you to attempt will not be so easy. I want you to ask Reiki, What is your purpose?

It is not an easy question.

My answer came much later in my Reiki career, long after I became a Reiki Master Teacher. It evolved within me as I continued thinking and rethinking how I wished to do my workshops and more importantly, the attunements. To find my final step in being claimed by Reiki, I wondered what Reiki's purpose was. When I knew that answer, I could then ask myself was there anything I could do to move my Reiki closer to Reiki's purpose?

After my meditation to her, I came away with the following answer. Divine Being, Deity, Spirit, Reiki, Universal Life Force, gave to us the gift of healing energy, to share, to use to help ourselves and others in every possible way that is in harmony with the people both giving and receiving that Energy.

To put it simply, use Reiki, spread Reiki, share Reiki, expand Reiki.

But what did that mean to me? As a practitioner and teacher, I thought did everything on my short list. What more could I do to further allow my students to transmit Reiki in the strongest possible way so they could become true agents of the Reiki Energy? What more could I do with my clients? I couldn't answer those questions. When I couldn't come up with anything additional that I could add to either my sessions or workshops to further Reiki's purpose, I sort of forgot about it. I was very comfortable with what I did and I trusted that when the answer was supposed to come, it would. Remember I said Universe works in her own time and her own way. And in her own time, she did.

I was attuning two nurses to Level 1. Nurses! Of all the professions one could be in that would help spread the peace and healing energy to as many people as possible, people who needed Reiki, a person in the medical field would be the absolute best. Standing behind my two students, centering myself before beginning their attunement, Spirit whispered, that extraneous thought that popped into my head without warning or reason. A simple idea came to me.

Why don't I attune each nurse to all the symbols? Technically, and I nit-pic now, that would mean I was attuning both of them to Level 3. Whatever energy, whatever level of intensity I and other Reiki Masters use, would now be available to each of my students, even though they didn't know they could call on that energy. But Reiki would know, wouldn't she? And their higher selves, their divine souls, they would also know.

This WAS a Level 1 workshop and I would not change that. That would be too blasphemous, even for me. I wouldn't say anything that was supposed to be said in higher-level workshops. There are certain things that even I, a nontraditional practitioner, would not do. And this I would not. They would leave with their Level 1 certificate. But those higher selves, those divine souls would know and maybe use that knowledge to upgrade their Level 1 to whatever the situation called for even though the regular selves of each nurse would be unaware.

As I attuned each student, I knew that by trusting my feelings as I went through the process, I was doing what I needed to in order to fulfill Reiki's purpose.

What I was doing felt right to me. I had chills in my face, my arms, my chest. I felt like I did that very first time I meditated to and entered Reiki's light.

I knew what I was doing was right for me.

"What if I was wrong?" you ask.

"What possible harm could I do if I was?" I answer. Only Reiki and I, along with their higher selves, would ever know. If I was wrong, and those higher energies never increased the intensity of my students' Reiki, would attuning them to the additional symbols cause any ill to them or others? I don't think so. And what if that whisper was totally within the realm of my imagination, invented by my subconscious in order to empower me to complete my journey to claiming Reiki as my own? What did I once say, "You must accept that the information you receive will be valid for you. No matter where the information comes from, no matter how vivid your imagination (and imagination it will be), she will not lie to you." Am I not just like you?

Since a large percentage of my students were nurses, from then on, I attuned all the nurses in this manner. Not once did I think I was doing anything incorrect or counter to the gift of Reiki.

Empowering me by her Wisdom, so did Reiki.

Chasing away my last doubts, so did Reiki.

Sealing forever my trust and belief in her, in my personal relationship with her, so did Reiki.

Do I suggest other Reiki Masters do the same? Of course not.

Do I suggest other Reiki Masters look into themselves and decide Reiki's purpose and if they are in harmony with it? Of course, yes.

And if they don't, will that make them any less of a Reiki Master or Reiki Master Teacher? No, no no and no! By being true to themselves and staying within their honor and integrity, they are doing Reiki as they feel Reiki must be done. We all have our own inner truth and to that should we be true.

Our own way, our own path, our own truth, each of us must find.

Now, if you wish, meditate to Reiki Energy or your symbol and ask the following:

What is your purpose?

(If need be, add) Is there anything I can do to move my Reiki closer to your purpose?

Tying Up Loose Ends

Loose ends, what wasn't said before but ought to have been. They weren't because they didn't relate directly to your being empowered by, or embraced by or claimed by Reiki. So they stayed where they were, hanging out in my mind, waiting their turn. Now it's their turn:

Reiki Lineage

The text was meant to build up your personal knowledge of Reiki by going to the source. By now, you should have the confidence to know that what you do is what you need to do, and you do it with Reiki's blessings. But there are several issues that might disenfranchise you, and pull you away from your personal Reiki. All these issues would be brought up by traditional practitioners. Most are minor - one may not be so I thought I would mention it.

Earlier, I said some practitioners believe if you don't do Reiki the way Mrs. Takata did, you aren't doing Reiki. The one issue that may come is this. A traditional practitioner might ask you, "What is your lineage?" That means they want to know if the person who attuned your Reiki Master was attuned by a Reiki Master who was attuned by a Reiki Master who was attuned to Reiki by one of the twenty-two Reiki Masters that Mrs. Takata attuned.

They want you know if you can trace your lineage in Reiki back to Mrs. Takata because she was attuned by a man who was attuned by Dr. Usui himself. Your Reiki heritage should, according to them, go back to the original Reiki Master, Dr. Usui.

The reason I avoid those discussions with a simple, "I don't know the lineage of my Reiki Master" is because the traditionalist would like us to believe that if the direct line leading from Mrs. Takata to you is broken, the Reiki you do is also broken. In other words, their Reiki is purer than yours.

You have almost completed a book written for one purpose, to show you many different ways of empowering yourself and your Reiki. You know what you are doing and why you are doing it. Why put ourselves in a position where someone will try to tear down our belief in Reiki in order to build up their own ego and their belief that their Reiki is better than ours?

You know by now, it can never be better. It can be different - but never better. All Reiki is Reiki. The difference is your Reiki is built around you and who you are. It is your personal Reiki. She has empowered you, she has embraced you, and she has claimed you. Their Reiki is built around Mrs. Takata. It is generic Reiki.

What possible difference could it make to Reiki the history of those who placed his/her hands on you and attuned you to the various levels? For me, the answer is none.

Responsibility

Who is responsible: for us, for our words, our deeds, our actions? We are. When we were born into this world, we enter with nothing and when we leave this world, we leave with nothing. All that we can hope for is that when we are gone, people will remember us for the kind of person we were. What kind of honor did we have, what kind of integrity did we have. Was our word our bond - or were we like all the other people who move from excuse to excuse, saying over and over, "I'm sorry, but it really wasn't my fault."

Sometimes, in speaking to clients who have seen other Reiki practitioners over the years, I hear about their upsets. One upset goes under the heading of things I think a Reiki practitioner should do, and I ask you to consider the following.

According to me, as Reiki practitioners, as healers, we have a responsibility to our clients. These responsibilities go beyond what happens during a session or workshop.

We must be available to our clients afterwards. If a client calls a day after the session and says they are having trouble grounding themselves, you cannot simply say you have no time and forget about it. If you really don't have time, then set up a time when the client can call you back.

If a client calls after a session or workshop for any reason, for any upset they have regarding Reiki, please, you must take the time to listen and advise them best you can. By now, you have a personal relationship with your Reiki; you have meditated to her and discovered what her purpose is. My purpose states to use Reiki to help others in every possible way that is in harmony with the people both giving and receiving her Energy. To help in every possible way. For me, that means I must be there for them if they need me to further their ability to use their Reiki in their best possible way. That is a responsibility I took on for myself. No one told me or suggested I create that responsibility. I just did because it felt right. I now ask you to take on your own responsibilities, whatever they are, as long as they are in harmony with what you have decided is Reiki's purpose. And if they are the same as mine, that's excellent.

A client once called me because a religious friend of hers, on hearing she was attuned to Reiki, told her how terrible that was, that Reiki was from the devil and the church didn't accept it. She went on and on, said my student, as her friend told her not to tell anyone or practice it because it wasn't Deity's work. I think we spoke for close to an hour before my student became comfortable again with what she hoped to do with Reiki and told me that she would just ignore the naysayers.

I believe it is your responsibility to be where you said you would be, at the time you agreed on to see a client if you travel to them or make sure you are ready to see the client if they come to you.

I believe it your responsibility to speak your truth to your client (or student) and when you don't know say so.

I believe it your responsibility to be the best practitioner you can regardless of how you feel: tired, bored, lonely, anxious etc. You represent Reiki and since she is always there for us, you have to be always there for her.

I ask you to do one last meditation. Meditate to Reiki and ask her what personal responsibilities you should accept. After all the work you did or are doing in establishing your personal relationship to Reiki, please do not overlook this loose end.

Conclusion

By the time you have reached this point, you have all the

building blocks you need to create your own foundation for your house of Reiki. You know how I deepened my relationship with Reiki. You know I was empowered by her, embraced by her and how I was claimed her. I have said many times that what works for me may not work for you. That was and still is true. But even if some of what I said is not within your comfort zone, you have the knowledge and the meditative skills to ask Reiki whatever questions you need answered in order to be empowered by her, embraced by her and claimed by her, and all within the confines of your own comfort level.

No matter where you are on the path of Reiki experience or the level of Reiki you have achieved, you were called to this modality when a need burned inside of you. This book was created because of conversations I had with people whose fire and passion for Reiki waned or was beginning to dim, and I wanted to avoid that feeling with as many people as I could.

After all I have said, I leave you with these last thoughts.

Reiki is part of Universe's generosity to all of us.

Reiki is. The more you use her, the more of Universe's generosity is placed on Mother Earth.

How you use Reiki is dwarfed by the fact that you use Reiki.

It is your gift.

Use it your own way.

Use it powerfully.

Use it well.

Use it often.

Robert can be reached at: WakingOurWorld@aol.com. He will respond to inquiries about private work, appearances, and further studies in empowering yourself to be the Reiki practitioner you wish to be. High volume may make it impossible to answer emails regarding opinions and reactions to this book.

AYNI
BOOKS

"Ayni" is a Quechua word meaning "reciprocity" – sharing, giving and receiving – whatever you give out comes back to you. To be in Ayni is to be in balance, harmony and right relationship with oneself and nature, of which we are all an intrinsic part. Complementary and Alternative approaches to health and well-being essentially follow a holistic model, within which one is given support and encouragement to move towards a state of balance, true health and wholeness, ultimately leading to the awareness of one's unique place in the Universal jigsaw of life – Ayni, in fact.